MW00677525

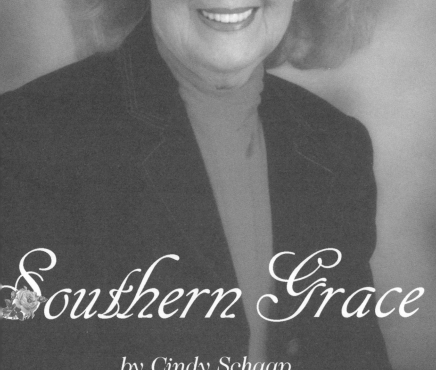

Southern Grace

by Cindy Schaap

© 2009
CHRISTIAN WOMANHOOD
8400 Burr Street
Crown Point, Indiana 46307
www.christianwomanhood.org
(219) 365-3202

ISBN: 978-0-9815087-9-5

CREDITS:
Layout and Design: Linda Stubblefield
Cover Consultant: Carol Worley
Proofreaders: Rena Fish, Jane Grafton, Diane Rykhus
Research: Valerie Morales

Tea Party Photo: Katie Banek
Courtesy of Kristal Slager

All Scripture references used in this book
are from the King James Bible.

Printed and Bound in the United States

Dedication

*T*his book is lovingly dedicated to my husband's and my grandchildren: the children of our daughter, Jaclynn Weber, and her husband Todd

Lyndsay Alana Weber
born March 18, 2005

Raymond Jack Weber
born August 19, 2006

Alexys Marlene Weber
born September 13, 2008

and to our grandbaby due to be born in the spring of 2009 to our son, Ken Schaap, and his wife Candace, and to all of our grandchildren yet to come.

I wanted you to know how blessed you are to have a great-grandmother like Beverly Hyles and how blessed I feel to have her for my mother.

I love you!

Grammy

Other Books by Cindy Schaap

A Meek and Quiet Spirit
Lessons for Wives and Mothers
from Women in the New Testament

A Wife's Purpose

A Peaceful Marriage

Bright Side Planner/Journal

From the Coal Mines to the Gold Mines
An Authorized Biography of Russell Anderson

Living on the Bright Side
Principles for Lasting Joy, Especially for Ladies

Silk and Purple
Lessons for Wives and Mothers
from Women in the Old Testament

The Fundamental Man
An Authorized Biography of Jack Frasure Hyles

The Path to a Woman's Happiness

Training Kings and Queens

With Gratitude

I must thank Rena Fish and Jane Grafton for their help in proofreading this manuscript. Rena has been my proofreader for nearly all of my books, and I value her input and advice. Jane is the managing editor of *Christian Womanhood*, and I am grateful for her diligence in her work.

Linda Stubblefield has been the layout designer and typesetter for all of my books. She is my assistant editor at Christian Womanhood, and she is a tireless worker.

I thank Valerie Morales and Debi Young for sharing information and input.

I am grateful to my husband and pastor, Dr. Jack Schaap, for all of the ways he has encouraged me and enabled me to honor my parents and carry on their legacy.

Table of Contents

Unit III
Southern Grace and Charm

Unit IV
Southern Grace and Homemaking

Unit V
Southern Grace: A Biographical Sketch

Introduction

*M*y mother, Beverly Hyles, was a pastor's wife for 53 years. She was my pastor's wife for the first 41 years of my life. For 41 years, she was the pastor's wife of what became a megachurch, the First Baptist Church of Hammond, Indiana. For these reasons alone, her life deserves to be recorded in a book, but that is not the main reason I am writing this book.

Mom has said she enjoys the more anonymous life she has lived since my father's death and the quieter life she has led following the end of her role as a pastor's wife. She does not miss being on a pedestal. My mother is not the type of person who would particularly desire a book to be written about her.

During the year 2008, Beverly Hyles has had a battle with Stage I breast cancer. This is a battle which she has fought calmly and bravely in typical Beverly Hyles' style. I suppose no one likes to associate the words "Mom" and "cancer" together, but that health crisis is not the main reason I am writing this book.

On February 14, 2009, my mother will have completed 80 years of living. This is quite a milestone, and yes, it does cause me to cherish even more every opportunity I have to see my mother's face and to hear her voice. Yet my mom looks as beautiful and acts as strong as she ever has, and Mom is from a family that tends to live into their nineties. That is my hope and prayer for my mother. The age factor is not the main reason I am writing this book. I am writing this book for two reasons:

1. **I want to bring honor to my mother**. I want those thousands of people who love my mother to know her from my perspective. Even more than that, I want my mother, Beverly Hyles, to know and to see in print my perspective and my heart about her as my mom.

Beverly Hyles is a humble lady. Though I believe my mother has developed a healthy sense of self-worth, I don't believe she has ever seen herself as those who admire her see her. This book is an effort to convey to her how I see her, and hopefully, as she looks in the mirror of this book, she will see herself as I do.

2. **I want to establish my mother's life as a pattern for the future generations of young ladies to follow.** My father went to Heaven on February 6, 2001. One month later on March 7, 2001, my husband became my father's successor as pastor of the First Baptist Church of Hammond, Indiana.

As a pastor's wife of eight years, hardly a week passes without a young lady's coming to me and asking me how to succeed as a wife, mother, homemaker, and Christian lady. I sense that these ladies are looking for some new and complicated answer, and for the most part, I have none.

As I have reflected on the life of Beverly Hyles, I have realized that her life is the pattern for which these young ladies are seeking. Mom's life is a pattern for success as a pastor's wife, a mother, a homemaker, and a Christian lady. Yet my mother's life is not filled with the new, the trendy, or the complicated. Hers has been a simple and structured life of the old school. Mom's life teaches us that quiet discipline and simple consistency are the infallible keys which unlock the door to success. Beverly Hyles' life portrays the value of grace, femininity, and the traditional role of women.

I am the senior editor of the Christian Womanhood Magazine and Publications. Our ministry compiled and published a book entitled *Pattern for Living* for young girls to learn how to be successful godly women. The book *Southern Grace* is another attempt to give young girls a pattern for success as a godly woman. Only this time the pattern is a living role model, Mrs. Beverly Hyles.

My mom's life has not been without failure. In her humility, she would be the first one to wish for that to be realized. Yet the panoramic view of my mother's life shows the achievements of a lady who has been a worldwide influence without ever leaving her traditional role. Mom's life is a pattern of what God can do with a woman who is dedicated to serving Him without putting grace and femininity behind her.

Purposefully, I have strived to portray my mother's life in a point-by-point fashion. My hope is that young ladies of generations to come will read this book and learn how to succeed as traditional, Biblical women of femininity and grace. My desire is that my daughter Jaclynn, my daughter-in-law Candace, and their daughters will learn what a pattern their grandmother set forth for them.

This past summer God clearly showed me that He wanted a book to be written about Beverly Hyles and that He wanted me to author it. God impressed on me to title this book *Southern Grace*. I have shared this title with several others who know and love Mom. Each has responded with a similar reply, "Aaaaah! That's perfect. I love the title!" Why have they responded in this way? Because my mother is most known for her Southern drawl and most beloved for her graciousness.

My prayer is that God will use this book to help the ladies who read it to return to graciousness and to return to femininity.

My prayer is also that my mother will see in the pages of *Southern Grace* the great love and admiration I have for her reflected from my heart.

It has been a great joy to write and publish this book about my mother, Beverly Hyles. Thank you for sharing this book and my joy with me.

"The aged women likewise, that they be in behaviour as becometh holiness, not false accusers, not given to much wine, teachers of good things. [4]That they may teach the young women to be sober, to love their husbands, to love their children, [5]To be discreet, chaste, keepers at home, good, obedient to their own husbands, that the word of God be not blasphemed. [7]In all things shewing thyself a pattern of good works: in doctrine, shewing uncorruptness, gravity, sincerity." (Titus 2:3–5, 7)

Southern Grace
& Family

The Hyles family

Front left to right: Linda and Cindy
Middle: Pastor and Mrs. Hyles and David
Back: Becky

1

Southern Grace
Is Bringing Your Child to Jesus

"*I*'m saved! I'm saved!" I remember shouting as I ran down the hallway and down the main flight of stairs of our quad-level house in Munster, Indiana. I was five years old. My mother had taken me to the living room couch and told me how I could trust Jesus as my Saviour. I proceeded to ask Jesus into my heart. I don't remember much else about this time, but I remember that I was very excited, and I appreciate my mother for sharing the Gospel with me at an early age.

At nine years of age, I began to doubt my salvation. My 11-year-old sister had recently made sure of her salvation. I awoke during the middle of the night on a Sunday night, afraid that I was not saved. I was afraid if the Lord came back during the night, I would be left behind.

I ran across the hall to my parents' bedroom and woke my mother. I told her my doubts and fears, and she went over the plan of salvation with me again. I prayed the sinner's prayer with her, and that is the time to which I attribute my salvation. I probably was saved at age five, but the first time that I remember understanding the plan and carefully applying its truths to my own life was that night at the age of nine. It was April 19, 1968.

After praying the sinner's prayer with my mother, I proceeded to my father's side of the bed. Dad went over the Gospel with me again, and I prayed again. I teasingly say that I was saved twice in one night! I don't know if my dad wanted to be sure that I understood it this time, or if he was so tired on a late Sunday night after preaching that he didn't realize what had happened, but I prayed the prayer to accept Christ with both parents that night! Still I attribute my salvation to my mother, and I always have. How can we thank enough the person who led us to the Lord?

Mark 10:13-16 says, *"And they brought young children to him, that he should touch them: and his disciples rebuked those that brought them. [14]But when Jesus saw it, he was much displeased, and said unto them, Suffer the little children to come unto me, and forbid them not: for of such is the kingdom of God. [15]Verily I say unto you, Whosoever shall not receive the kingdom of God as a little child, he shall not enter therein. [16]And he took them up in his arms, put his hands upon them, and blessed them."*

Who do you think the "they" were who brought these children to Jesus? Don't you imagine that they were parents, mothers in particular, who had heard that Jesus *"...cometh into the coasts of Judæa"*? (Mark 10:1) These mothers had probably heard about Jesus, and their thoughts were not for themselves. They wanted their children to have a chance to see Jesus while He was in the nearby area. Can you imagine how excited these mothers must have been to introduce their particular child to Jesus?

"Jesus, this is Meaghan," or "Jesus, this is Trent." All mothers know the pride they feel when they show off their child, especially to someone they admire. Maybe these mothers had prepared a treat for Jesus and had given it to their child to present to Him.

Who do you think the "those that brought them" were who suffered rebuke from the disciples? I believe they were mothers whose minds were not on what others might think, or what the consequences might be. Their heartfelt responsibility was to get their child to Jesus.

Jesus was displeased—not with the little children, nor with the mothers who had brought them. He was displeased with those who rebuked the mothers. He was displeased with those who said, "These children are too young to be brought to Jesus."

Many in this generation say, "This child is too young to be saved." Or "There are just a bunch of little kids on that bus route." But Jesus saw children as the best kind of converts when He said, "...*Whosoever shall not receive the kingdom of God as a little child, he shall not enter therein.*"

What was the reward of the mothers who brought their children to Jesus? Jesus put His hand upon their children and blessed them, and I'm sure the mothers went away happy. Their goal was not to receive anything for themselves, but instead to receive it for their children.

As a 49-year-old mother and grandmother, I have lived a life that has been truly blessed. I have felt God's hand upon me and mine in a glorious way. But all of this blessing—every bit of it—was made possible on April 19, 1968. It was made possible by the

woman who brought me to Jesus as a little child.

I am thankful that my mother did not think I was too young to be brought to Jesus when I was five. I am thankful that my mother had it in her heart to introduce me to Jesus while I was young!

Graciousness—"being noticed for your kindness and courtesy." Surely one of the kindest things a mother can do is to bring her child to Jesus. How kind and gracious my mother was to me on that happy day when she introduced me to Jesus!

Genesis 44:34, *"For how shall I go up to my father, and the lad be not with me?..."*

2

Southern Grace
Is Being There for Your Children

*T*hough my mother is a quiet, unassuming woman, what I remember most about her in my childhood involves the words "being there." Mom was always there!

When I awoke in the morning, Mom was there with a good old-fashioned breakfast. Cereal or donuts were rarely the breakfast of Mom's choice. Instead, she prepared eggs (scrambled with cheese were my favorite), toast, and some type of breakfast meat. It seems like breakfast was always ready at the same time each morning. I don't recall ever going to church, like so many bus kids do, with nothing to eat. My day never began with low blood sugar and a hollow stomach.

During most of my school years, Mom picked me up and took me to school. For a short period of time, we carpooled with another family. When Mom did not take me to school, my last sight of her each morning was at the kitchen table. Some mornings she was reading the newspaper; most mornings she was reading her Bible.

From the first through the fifth grade, my first sight of Mom each afternoon was in the Lanier Public School parking lot. I would walk out the door of my grade school, look down the line-up of cars, and see the shadow of my mother. She was always beautiful, always the same, and always twisting her hair. Mom had a regular habit of taking several strands of hair and twisting them around her finger over and over. It was a habit I love. It was a habit that said, "There is your mother." It was an endearing habit!

One school day Mom did not come to pick me up right away, and there was a storm threatening on the horizon. I was terribly afraid of tornadoes—neurotically afraid of tornadoes.

On Rearing Children…

Don't overprotect.

Children learn by doing, so it is important to let them make their own mistakes.

— Beverly Hyles

Mom was rarely late anywhere she went—especially if it had to do with her children. In my mind if Mom was late, Mom wasn't coming. Our church organist and associate pastor's wife, Elaine Colsten, lived just one block from my school, so I ran to her house. She comforted me while my mother, who had arrived just a few minutes late, frantically tried to find me. I suppose my panic over a threatening storm illustrates what a fearful child I was, but it also illustrates one other thing. It illustrates how unaccustomed I was to my mother's not being there every time I looked for her—twisting her hair and waiting for me.

My mom became concerned that my carpool buddies and I might be getting into trouble during our high school years, so she resumed taking me and picking me up from school herself.

One November day of my junior year of high school, something happened that changed my life forever; I was not quite 16 years of age.

Mom said, "I have a meeting, and I may not be able to pick you up from school this afternoon. If I am not there when school finishes, ride in the carpool you used to ride in."

As it turned out, Mom was there waiting for me when I got out of school—twisting her hair.

It was the day before Thanksgiving, and the first snowfall of the year started on our way home from school. The driver of the carpool in which I almost rode that day swerved on the bridge of a snowy, slippery road toward an oncoming truck. A college-age young man met his eternity that day, and all of the other young people in the car were injured and taken to a hospital. Two of those injured were in critical condition. One of them was one of my best friends. Sharon Stromberg was in a coma and pronounced dead four times. Though she recovered after four months in the hospital, she was killed in a house fire a year later.

My dad took me to the hospital to visit Sharon that Wednesday evening before Thanksgiving. When I arrived home, I went to a window and watched the snow falling. I began to pray a prayer that went something like this:

"Dear Lord...

Today I almost saw You. If I had been in that carpool, I might have seen You today. If I had seen You, I would not have had much to say to You. You have given me so much, and I have given You very little in return.

Lord, I don't make a very good pastor's daughter. I don't make a very good daughter of a famous man. But today I quit trying. Today I ask You, Jesus, to live Your life through me and to be a pastor's daughter through me."

———

Mine was a simple prayer with not much faith behind it, but God answered the prayer of a nearly 16-year-old girl, and He changed my life! My sophomore year of high school I had been suspended from school for a day and had almost been expelled for a semester. My grades were faltering. I was too serious in my dating of a young man.

At the end of my junior year, I found myself with a straight "A" report card, 0 demerits, and having broken up with my boyfriend, with a commitment not to date seriously until college. The next man I would date seriously was Jack Schaap, who is now my husband.

I see that Wednesday evening in November and my little prayer as being one of the three or four major turning points in my life. Though I do not think any parent of those carpoolers was wrong for sending his or her child in a carpool, I often wonder what would have happened if Mom had not been there on that fateful day.

Sharon has been in Heaven since we were both 17. I have now lived 32 years beyond what she did. Those who know me might say that I have accomplished a lot in those 32 years. To some degree, I always feel I am accomplishing something for Sharon also. I also remind myself that none of those accomplishments would have taken place had my mother not been there—waiting in the line-up of cars and twisting her hair.

The youngest of four children, or as my parents would say, the baby of the family, I was born into our family when my mother was 30. I was the last child to leave the home and the one who longest prevented my parents from being empty nesters.

On Rearing Children...

Help your children dream great dreams.

Don't stifle any dreams they may have and be careful not to put them down.

— Beverly Hyles

During my senior year of high school, Mom started teaching part-time at Hyles-Anderson College. When I married and left the house, my mother began to do several things she had done little of in the past. She started traveling and speaking at ladies' meetings, she began writing books, she took up painting, and she made some music CDs. I appreciate so much that my mom did not stop her child rearing until her last child was out of the house. She was always there—whether it was for four children or just one—just for me. She had done so much mothering that when I left the home, a whole new world opened up to her. So many mothers do what **they** want while their children are young, frequently committing the keeping of their children's souls to daycare. Then when their children are grown, they lament the fact that they have regrets from their child-rearing years. Child rearing is not something they can recapture. Other opportunities would have still been available after the child-rearing years, but they have used them all up. They are not new and exciting to them.

I have observed that often the difference between a good lady and a great lady, or even a seemingly bad lady and a great lady, is simply a matter of priorities. My mom is a great lady who kept her priorities in order. I am thankful that my mom was there until the end of her child rearing—for me!

Not every mother can be beautiful—though mine is! Not every mother can be talented—though mine is! Not every mother can be smart—though mine is! But every mother can be there. Being there only takes one thing—it takes commitment. It takes being more committed to your loved one than to your beauty, your talent, or your brains. It takes being more committed to your children than to your own ambitions or finances.

"Mom, I am forever grateful for the mental image of your being there—waiting for me—sometimes just me—and twisting your hair!"

3

Southern Grace
Is Being a Committed Wife

*This poem was written by Cindy Schaap in honor
of her parents' fiftieth wedding anniversary.*

I once knew a man and a woman,
Committed were they to a cause.
Their marriage, not based just on romance,
Nor fortune, nor just man's applause.

Their vows were not casually spoken,
Not broken through so many years.
Sustained was their love through four children,
Through testings, sore trials, and tears.

Their ministry kept them together,
Yet often it took them apart,
To preach and to share with God's people,
To whom they had given their hearts.

Yet still through each new separation,
Their love yet continued to grow.
Their love was oft' fed and still nurtured,
In ways that e'en they didn't know.

Their theme was old-fashioned commitment;
It wasn't their nature to change.
They lived long in one house together;
To move would to them seem so strange.

So quickly the years passed right by them;
So busy were they doing right.
'Twas hard to believe how God used them,
And then came to them darkest night.

I watched them to see what would happen;
Their Heaven had now turned to Hell.
Would their love survive this new trial,
As if all were still going well?

This battle was brought to destroy them,
Yet more love this battle did send.
They thought they'd by all been forsaken,
But found they still had their best friend.

Their friendship and love had been growing
Through every trial and storm.
Now they still as one are together,
While sun shines and days grow more warm.

Their hearts are still knit with God's
    people;
They still give to them with great
    zest.
Yet they share a new bond together;
Their golden year has been their best.

Each season brings new disappoint-
    ments.
I trust in their love without fear.
I've seen that their love now has
    lasted
Through trials of 50 sweet years.

Their faithfulness to stay together,
The best of examples I've had.
I'm thankful for this loving couple;
I call them my own mom and dad.

*How to Stay Right
With Your Husband*

Convince him that you
love him
sincerely.

Praise him for the
little things.

Take care of his home,
his clothes, and his
meals.

— *Beverly Hyles*

On Building Your Man

Understand manhood in general;
in particular, your own man's manhood.

Understand that your man needs his work.

Understand that your man is made secure
by the loving intimacies of marriage.

Respect your man as a person.
He needs to know you think he is important.

Adapt to your man and his dreams.

— *Beverly Hyles*

Unit 2

Southern Grace
& the Ministry

The young Beverly Hyles

4

Southern Grace
Is Taking a Stand
and Being a Woman of Strength

*I*f there is anything I admire about my mother, it is her ability to be strong without losing her femininity. Women in the Bible such as Deborah and the Proverbs 31 woman teach us that strength is a virtue in a woman's life.

In 1959 God called my father to leave his and my mother's homeland of Dallas, Texas. They were leaving all of their family members. I am the youngest of four children, and I am the only child who was not born in Texas. I remember being told as a child that there were no other living cousins or relatives other than myself who had not been born in Texas. When Mom and Dad left Texas, they literally left their whole family.

They could not have moved to an area in the United States that was more different from Texas than Hammond, Indiana. In Texas, the people were more friendly and had last names like "Smith" and "Jones." In Hammond, Indiana, there was a strong Polish-Catholic influence, and the names were difficult to pronounce. Mom and Dad moved to Indiana with strong Southern accents, and the people had difficulty understanding them. They probably also had a difficult time understanding the cowboy boots and the ten-gallon hat that my dad wore around town for several years after he moved "up north." The weather in Indiana could be very cold and snowy, and it had many extremes. Mom and Dad were used to the more mild weather of Texas.

There was a Baptist church on nearly every corner in Texas, whereas Northwest Indiana was predominantly Catholic.

Dad came to Hammond, Indiana, to accept the pastorate of the First Baptist Church in that city. The First Baptist Church was a very formal church. The pastor before my father wore a tuxedo with tails and a boutonniere when he preached every Sunday morning. There was no song leader in the church; the congregational singing was led by a pipe organ. Much of the church business was conducted by the many committees the church had.

When Jack Hyles took the pastorate, the church was introduced to a fast talking, fiery Southern preacher. Dad was uncomfortable in a tuxedo and tails. He rared back and preached on evangelism and against sin. He was exceedingly uncomfortable with a group of committees telling him how to run his church. He was married to a beautiful lady who was six months pregnant with her fourth child. That child was this author.

First Baptist Church was a rich church. Many of the richest businessmen in town attended this church and gave their tithes to it. My mother grew up in an upper-middle-class home and had been materially comfortable all of her life. On the other hand, my father grew up extremely poor. Though he had a passion for all people, he had a hot passion for two groups of people—the lost and the poor. He loved the people whom Jesus loved.

Soon great strife arose in the church over primarily two issues: Brother Hyles' policies on reaching the poor and his fiery preaching against sin.

There was a lengthy and hot battle between the rich people and those they influenced and my father. Somewhere, right in the middle of this battle, I was born.

On Taking a Stand for Right…

You will never be sorry
if you choose
to stand for
what is right.

– Beverly Hyles

The rich wanted to keep their buildings and their church, but they did not want to keep their new preacher—unless he agreed to stop busing poor children into their services. Dad stood firm in his decision to remain where he believed God had called him. It was not that Dad and Mom were not homesick for their homeland and their family. They would have loved to have returned from whence they came. But their stand was with doing the will of God and in following God rather than man. Their stand was also with the lost and the poor!

The battle grew nasty. One evening someone even set our house on fire. There was a lot of yelling during church business meetings. People also stood and screamed and threatened the preacher.

After several months of severe stress and fighting, a vote was taken, and my father won the vote. My father stayed, the bus kids stayed, and the rich people left with their tithes. Many people whom those rich people had influenced also left. First Baptist Church was basically starting over. Our church died in a way and was gloriously resurrected under the pastorate of my father.

How would it feel to leave your entire family and the only homeland you have ever known at the age of 30? How would it feel to move with three children and a fourth one on the way and to be greeted by people who seemed more like foreigners than fellow American citizens? How would it feel to be greeted with hostility, threats, and rejection? How does a woman stay poised, gracious, and beautiful under such circumstances? Why does a woman stay and follow under such distress? The answer is that such a woman possesses a supernatural combination of grace and strength!

The next ten years of Mom and Dad's life seemed relatively calm. I was just a tiny girl learning to walk, starting school, and becoming a junior-age child, so I was basically unaware of the daily sacrifices I'm sure my parents were making as a church under their watch care began to rebuild and grow at an amazingly fast pace.

The next time I remember noticing my mother's strength was in the early 1970s. This was the time when Dad got the vision to start Christian schools—first a junior high and a high school, then a grade school, and after these, a college.

I went to public school through the fifth grade. Dad was becoming increasingly concerned with the direction of the public schools in Munster, Indiana, where we lived. Out of love for his children, he took on the extreme burden of starting and administrating Christian schools. Out of love for his country, he added the more difficult burden of starting a Bible college for preachers. Dad often teased and said something like this, "If you hate somebody and want them to die a slow, miserable death, don't shoot them. Talk them into starting a Christian school."

In 1970 Dr. Elmer Towns visited our church on a Sunday morning and declared First Baptist Church to be the "World's Largest Sunday School." I was eleven years old. In 1971, Hammond Baptist Schools were started with grades 6 through 12. I was going into sixth grade. My sister Linda was an eighth grader, and my brother was a junior in high school. My sister Becky was a freshman at Tennessee Temple College of Chattanooga, Tennessee.

In 1972 Hyles-Anderson College was started. Somewhere during those years Dad ceased in my mind to be just "Dad." My father was a nationally known pastor who possessed great fame, and the Hyles family no longer felt like the usual family. I believe that all of us—my parents, all three of my siblings, and myself—began to feel added stress and pressure on our lives. Life was good, but never completely normal after that time.

I remember even then wondering how my mother handled all of the extra demands on my father's time. Now as the pastor's wife of the same church my father once pastored, I wonder even more. One can never completely understand the path of another; yet I believe I am as uniquely qualified as anyone to understand my mother. My mother was married to a visionary, as am I. My mother was a simple person, of sorts, as am I. She loved simple things like housekeeping, gardening, and routine. But after 1970, nothing was ever completely simple in my mother's life again. I understand now more than ever that each new vision my father brought home to share must have brought some amount of disquiet to my mother's heart. How did she handle all those overwhelming moments? How did she stay on track when tempted to quit? My mother possessed a supernatural combination of grace and strength.

As I said, after 1970 nothing was completely normal again for the Hyles family. During the 1980s, the attacks on our family began. Because we were a well-known family in many circles, our sins and failures were well-publicized and scrutinized. None of the Hyles children are perfect, myself included, and there was much to be discussed about our family. I know this must have been a grief of mind to my mother—probably her greatest grief. What mother likes to hear her child criticized, and publically at that! True or untrue, deserved or undeserved, public gossip of one's family tears at a mother's heart. Yet I never saw my mother crumble; I never saw her falter in her faithfulness to her church or home duties.

In 1989 my father was attacked. I was very close to my father. I waited for him late after every evening service. I knew him and his habits as well as almost anyone. It was hard to see his character attacked. I believed in him then, and though he has been in Heaven since February 2001, I believe in him now more than ever. If I ever saw my mom come through and take a stand, it was during this particular attack. Her stand with my father made all the difference in the world to our church and to my father personally.

I began to pray after the worst of that attack was over a prayer from Psalm 90:15, *"Make us glad according to the days wherein thou hast afflicted us, and the years wherein we have seen evil."*

God answered my prayer! My dad lived 12 years after this attack began. Some time around the time the attacks died down, Dad asked God to give him ten more years to pastor our church. Dad didn't live much longer than that, but God gave Dad what he asked for. He had ten more years. I remember them as some of the sweetest, happiest, and most "normal" of my parents' lives. God answered my dad's prayer, and He answered mine!

In the year 2000, Dad began to suffer more and more with back pain. That back pain turned into a heart attack in January 2001 and a diagnosis of a blocked aorta, a serious heart condition.

Dad was in the hospital for a week after his heart attack and after his diagnosis. Then he went to Heaven. What I remember most about my mom during that week of diagnosis and surgery is her strength. She was by my father's bedside all day, every day. He had become her life.

I could see a tenseness in her eyes at times. There were times when I knew she was praying. But I never saw her panic, and I never saw her change much from what was the routined Beverly Hyles.

Dad went into surgery on Monday morning, February 5, 2001. It was a surgery that the doctors doubted would be successful. Neither did they believe Dad's body was strong enough to take the stress of such a serious surgery. But we as a family clung to hope. Hope was all we had, and it was to hope that we would cling. It was the gift of hope that made our last days and hours with my father happy ones. Dad's body lost strength during that week, but his spirit never weakened.

As Dad was rolled into surgery, our family followed my mother to the waiting room with strength and dignity. It was a strength I did not feel, but I followed what I saw in my mother.

The doctors were right. Dad's body was not strong enough to handle the surgery. He had another heart attack on the operating table. He never regained consciousness. Just before a decision had to be made to unplug his life support, Dad's heart officially stopped beating on the morning of February 6, 2001. All of that time Mom seemed pained, but strong.

The next week was filled with the responsibilities surrounding the family of a famous person, including the responsibility to gently let the nation and the world know that their friend had died. We began the tricky stage of guarding our family privacy, carrying our deep grief, and letting thousands of others, some who were even strangers to us, have their chance to say "goodbye." All of this Mom handled with dignity.

There was a funeral on Friday evening, February 9, for all around the country and the world who wished to come. Another funeral was held on Saturday morning, February 10, for those beloved church members only. Our family, of course, attended both of them. Mom spoke at Dad's funeral. Her words were well-chosen, appropriate for the man my father was, and they were strong.

The burial ceremony was private, just for our family. I recall all of our family standing around Dad's coffin, viewing what was left of him. The funeral home director asked if we were ready to have the casket closed.

My mind was whirling! How do you say "yes" to such a question? How do you say, "Yes, I am ready never to see my loved one again in this life"? How do you say, "Yes, I am finished looking at the face of my father or husband"? A feeling of uncertainty and panic began to rise inside of me. Before I had a chance to nurse these damaged emotions, I heard a strong and definite, "Yes, we are ready." It was my mother. And the casket was closed. We all followed my mother's lead and walked away with a strength and dignity we did not really feel.

How do you retain your dignity when your family is publicly attacked? How do you retain your dignity when your husband is personally attacked? How do you retain your dignity when one of the strongest leaders you have ever known is weak, sick, and dying before your eyes? How do you retain the dignity of your loved one through two very public funerals and a burial ceremony? You retain such dignity through a supernatural combination of grace and strength. This is a strength and a grace which I have always known my mother, Beverly Hyles, to possess.

On Handling Crises…

Don't deny your feelings. Feelings are not wrong.

Don't be afraid to ask God "Why?"
But realize He is under no obligation to tell you why.

Don't get angry at God when the problem isn't fixed.
Time is not an issue with God.

Realize that you may not feel God's presence.

Realize that trials come, not that we can be delivered to be
comfortable, but that we can be made into comforters.

Don't quit your service for God and for others.

Watch your health.

— *Beverly Hyles*

5

Southern Grace
Is Using Your Talent for the Lord

I love my mother's singing voice. She has a strong, clear soprano voice, and she possesses a great deal of pathos in her voice. The pathos is what sets her voice apart from others. She sings as if she has lived what she is singing. She sings sincerely and with feeling.

As a junior-age girl, Beverly Hyles sang in a girls' trio at her church. One of the trio members was Libby Sumrall, the pastor's daughter. This afforded Beverly the opportunity to spend much time in her pastor's home. The pastor's wife became a role model to Beverly. She made being a pastor's wife look good to Beverly.

As a young teenager, Beverly continued to sing in a church trio with Libby Sumrall and Marguerite Stevenson. Marguerite was used by God to influence Beverly's future husband to surrender to preach.

In high school, Mom struggled with the choice to pursue music or art. Though later years would prove that she had great artistic ability, Mom chose to make music her pursuit in high school. This was a great choice. Mom used her music as she sang before the congregations where her husband pastored. Before my father preached his first sermon at First Baptist Church of Hammond, Indiana, an expectant mother stood up to sing. That expectant mother was my mother. She was six months pregnant with me. Looking beautiful (as I have been told by eyewitnesses), Mom sang "There is a Balm in Gilead," and the words to that beautiful song are as follows:

Refrain:

"There is a balm in Gilead
To make the wounded whole;
There is a balm in Gilead
To heal the sin-sick soul."

Verse 1

"Sometimes I feel discouraged
And think my work's in vain,
But then the Holy Spirit
Revives my soul again."

Verse 2

"If you can't preach like Peter,
If you can't pray like Paul,
You just tell the love of Jesus,
And say, 'He died for all.' "

Verse 3

"Don't ever feel discouraged,
For Jesus is your friend.

And if you lack for knowledge,
He'll never refuse to lend."[1]

———

During high school, Beverly sang in both the church and school choirs, and she often sang at assemblies and at the teen canteen. On one particular occasion, she was chosen to represent Sunset High School at an all-city program at the teen canteen. A dance was to follow the program; and though Beverly planned to leave before the dance, she knew that she had no business being there. Beverly got up to sing and could not remember her words. She went behind a curtain, where others encouraged her to go out and try again. She tried again and forgot her words a second time. She tried a third time and forgot the words again. Finally, she sang another more familiar song. The audience was laughing, and among those laughing was a young man named Jack Hyles. The following Sunday an embarrassed and more humble Beverly Slaughter went forward at Hillcrest Baptist Church. She then promised God that she would give her voice to sing for Him. She would not use her talent for the world.[2]

1. **Graciousness is dedicating your talent to the Lord.** As mentioned in the previous paragraph, an embarrassing moment at a school dance motivated Mom to dedicate her singing voice to be solely used for the Lord. It also motivated her to move forward at a Sunday evening service and make this commitment public. Mom made this commitment, and she kept it. She never again used her voice for anything other than the Lord's work; and she did truly use her voice. Mom's was not a buried talent. It was a talent used over and over again in any way that she was asked.

2. Graciousness is being humble about your talent. Mom sang at nearly every wedding in the churches where my father pastored, and she sang at mine. She sang a duet with the prayer song entitled "Keep Us One," and she also sang "Take Our Life, Lord." In fact, Mom sang at the weddings of all four of her children.

Not only did she sing at most weddings, but she also sang at most every funeral. At one particular funeral which took place in a local funeral home, Mom took me with her. She normally went alone, but she could not find a babysitter. I was about seven years old, as I recall. I remember what a tiny humble funeral it was and that Mom hardly knew the man. As a child, what struck me most about this funeral was the fact that I saw a dead person for the very first time. As an adult, I realized what a humble task it had been for my mother to make herself available for funeral after funeral—sometimes for people she barely knew.

Mom never acted like she had obtained star status as a singer, though she certainly had the talent usually associated with stardom. She never had a hard time getting along with other singers. She never charged for her singing. She just humbly took every opportunity she had to sing. She sang many a Friday afternoon at local nursing homes for the residents there.

3. Graciousness is keeping your talent in the right priority. When I reflect on the years of my mother's life, I realize what a truly talented person she has been in almost every area. She is a great cook and decorator. She excels in some of the most coveted areas of talent including being a singer, an author, a nationally known conference speaker, and an artist.

Yet Mom was never known by her talent. She was known as a wife and mother. Most of these talents she did not pursue until I (the baby of four children) was nearly grown. It was when I was in college that I first recall Mom's pursuing her speaking, writing, and painting. She also began to do her first musical recordings at this time.

Mom has written four books: *I Feel Precious to God*; *Marred Vessels in the Potter's Hands*; *Life, as Viewed from the Goldfish Bowl*; and *Woman, the Assembler*.

Mom has made five musical recordings. Among the songs she has recorded is her favorite song, "Jesus Is the Sweetest Name I Know."

Chorus:

> "Jesus is the sweetest name I know,
> And He's just the same as His lovely name,
> And that's the reason why I love Him so;
> Oh, Jesus is the sweetest name I know."

Verse 1:

> "There have been names that I have loved to hear,
> But never has there been a name so dear
> To this heart of mine, as the name divine,
> The precious, precious name of Jesus."

Verse 2:

> "There is no name in earth or heav'n above,
> That we should give such honor and such love
> As the blessed name, let us all acclaim,
> That wondrous, glorious name of Jesus."

Verse 3:
> "And some day I shall see Him face to face
> To thank and praise Him for His wondrous grace,
> Which He gave to me, when He made me free,
> The blessed Son of God called Jesus."[3]

———

Mom has a collection of many beautiful paintings she has done. She has also shared many of those paintings with family and friends. She has been generous in donating her paintings for worthy causes, such as big promotion days at churches.

Yet most of these accomplishments were not done until her children were grown. Mom kept her talents in proper priority by humbly using her talent for the Lord in as many ways as she could, and yet also, by waiting until her children were cared for before she accomplished anything noteworthy regarding her talent.

Mom is most famous for the traditional Christmas song, "Sweet Little Jesus Boy," which she sang every Christmas at the First Baptist Church of Hammond, Indiana, for over 40 years and a total of 55 years if you include the years she sang it at Miller Road Baptist Church in Garland, Texas. I will end this chapter by printing the words to this song. Anyone who has followed Mom and her singing ministry would not feel a chapter on Mom's talent complete without reviewing these precious words.

Sweet Little Jesus Boy
> "Sweet little Jesus Boy,
> They made you be born in a manger.

Sweet little Holy Child,
Didn't know who You was
Didn't know You'd come to save us, Lord,
    to take our sins away.
Our eyes was blind; We couldn't see—
We didn't know who You was."

"Long time ago You was born,
    born in a manger low,
Sweet little Jesus Boy.
The world treat You mean, Lord,
Treat me mean too,
But please, Sir, forgive us, Lord,
We didn't know 'twas You.
Sweet little Jesus Boy,
Born long time ago.
Sweet little Holy Child,
And we didn't know who You was."[4]

[1] African-American spiritual

[2] Cindy Schaap, *A Fundamental Man* (Hammond: Hyles Publications, 1998) 83-84.

[3] Lela Long, "Jesus Is the Sweetest Name I Know," *Songs and Hymns of Revival* (Santa Clara: North Valley Publications, n.d.) 407.

[4] Robert MacGimsey, "Sweet Little Jesus Boy," New York: Carl Fischer Music Publishing Company, 1934.

Beverly Hyles performing at a Christmas concert at Daley Plaza in Chicago

6

$\mathcal{S}$outhern $\mathcal{G}$race
Is Faithfulness and Dedication

$\mathcal{T}$hough my mom was and is a very private person, I know that she walks with God and has walked with Him for many years.

I attended school at a public school near my home from first through fifth grades. I often walked to school. One of my favorite memories of childhood is walks to and from school down the streets of our safe and lovely neighborhood in our small all-American town of Munster, Indiana. I have always loved being outside during nice weather, and I must admit that I have always enjoyed being alone. I usually walked to and from school alone. I'm private like my mother, I guess, or perhaps we're just comfortable with ourselves.

All of that to say this: I rarely left home without one of the last sights I saw being my mother reading her Bible at the kitchen table. Occasionally, she was reading the newspaper. I have teased that those must have been the days when she was feeling less spiritual. Actually, I realize that she was either finished reading her Bible, or she was about to begin. That is my mom—consistent with her Bible, consistent and predictable about pretty much everything.

I also witnessed my mother reading her Bible as I would pass her bedroom in the evening. Frequently, I would see her sitting up in bed and enjoying a snack of either an apple, peanut butter and crackers, or both. I was amused when I passed my mother having her evening devotional time and snack. She seemed to be delighting in both her time in the Bible and in her snack.

My mother was often left alone because of my father's busy schedule and his traveling. Yet she rarely seemed lonely. Mom found pleasure in simple things. I believe this is one of her greatest virtues. Though she lived a complicated life as the wife of a megachurch pastor and that life afforded her many beautiful material possessions, she was not extravagant. She was able to find pleasure in the simple and the common; she delighted in them. This kept her on common and simple ground during an uncommon and complicated life.

Just this past evening, as my husband was out of town preaching, I enjoyed a snack of a few graham crackers as I sat up in my bed reading. Though I missed my husband, I was delighting in my snack (probably a little too much) and in the book I was reading on the love of God. I thought of my mother. I am grateful for the way I am able to emulate her life, and I am thankful for hers and my father's love of little things. I am exceedingly grateful that I inherited that simplicity from both of them.

Mom was also an avid reader of self-help books. It has been said that a person will be the same one year from now, except for the people he meets and the books he reads. My mother sought wisdom through her reading and not just entertainment—again a practice that she passed on to me. The wisdom of my mother's reading showed. Mom's reading enhanced her walk with God, rather than detracting from it.

I recall sitting beside a lovely table in the master bedroom of my parents' house and seeing a small sheet of paper which said "Prayer List" at the top. Nosily, I grabbed that paper and began to read it. I recall seeing the name "Cindy" on it. My heart soared. I'm sure that I knew my mother prayed for me before that moment. But there is something about actually seeing your name on someone else's prayer list, especially when it is someone dear. I don't believe I have ever shared with my mother how much that moment meant to me. I wish we all realized how much it can mean to our children and to others to know we are praying for them. I have no doubt that my mother is a prayer warrior and continues to be so, even into this her eightieth year!

It is a dedicated walk with God that allows someone to be as faithful as my mother has been.

- My mother was faithful to her husband. She was married for over 55 years, until my father passed away on February 6, 2001.
- My mother was faithful to her children. She was a stay-at-home mother while she reared all four of her children.
- My mother was faithful as a daughter. She cared for her mother in her home for over a dozen years until Eva Slaughter's death.
- My mother was faithful as a pastor's wife. She hardly ever missed a church service.

- My mother was faithful as a Sunday school teacher. She taught eighth grade girls for nearly 40 years.
- My mother was faithful as a choir member. She sat on the front row of the choir for all her years as a pastor's wife.
- My mother is faithful as a soul winner. She was actively involved in ministries like the nursing home ministry while she was a pastor's wife.
- My mother is faithful as a friend.
- My mother is faithful as a neighbor. My dad didn't get to know our neighbors as well because of his busy schedule. Yet Mom was close to many of our neighbors. Mom shopped in the same grocery store for 40 years, the entire time she lived in Munster, Indiana. The grocery clerks knew and admired my mother because of her impeccable and feminine appearance and her gracious manner.

As a Wife

My husband and I were able to spearhead the celebration of my parents' fiftieth wedding anniversary. The men on our full-time church staff helped us to plan a grand party for them. Mom and Dad were driven to that celebration in a 1941 Dodge exactly like one they had owned in the early years of their marriage.

My parents renewed their vows in the tiny church building where they had served during one of their first pastorates. This building had been moved to the Hyles-Anderson College campus, the campus of the Bible college where my dad was chancellor. My husband officiated in the renewal of Mom and Dad's wedding vows. Afterward, a first-class meal and reception had been planned. What a wonderful evening it was! I wish that everyone could have a part in his/her mom and dad's renewal of their wedding vows. The faithfulness of my mother granted me that rare privilege.

As a Daughter

My grandmother Eva Slaughter became sort of a recluse after my grandfather died. She got to the point where she never left her house. "Mamaw," as we called her, was married to a man who had built a rather affluent business. Their house was in an upper-middle-class neighborhood. After Papaw's death, that neighborhood began to decline, and safety became an issue for my grandmother. For these reasons, Mom and Dad decided to move Mamaw to Indiana to live with them. I was a senior in high school when Mamaw came to live with us. She came to us in her early eighties and stayed in our home until a few months right before her death at the age of 95.

Eva Slaughter was the kind of mother who would give her family the shirt off her back, so to speak. She sewed beautiful dresses for her daughter Beverly, and she was an excellent cook and homemaker. Eva was not an expressive person. Her works were the way that she expressed love. Because of this, Mamaw was not very expressive to my mom in all the years she took care of her. Mom loved her and diligently cared for her without receiving a lot of love and appreciation. This care displayed to me my mom's excellent character, as well as her obedience and love. Mom cared for Mamaw until her very last months, when it became physically impossible for Mom to care for her. At this point, Mamaw was moved to a suite adjacent to the Hyles-Anderson College clinic, and Mom visited her faithfully.

As a Pastor's Wife

Eight years ago, one month after my father went to Heaven, my husband was voted in to replace my dad in his former pastorate. For eight years I have walked somewhat in my mother's shoes as a pastor's wife. There, of course, are differences. I became the pastor's wife at the age of 41 with my only two children about to leave the nest. Jaclynn was 19, and Kenny was 16. My mom was 30 when she became the pastor's wife of First Baptist Church of Hammond, Indiana. As I have already mentioned, she was an expectant mother. She was six months along with me. She was also the mother of three other children: Becky, age seven; David, age five; and Linda, age two. She became a pastor's wife at a much busier stage of life. She also left her home state of Texas after 30 years to become a citizen of the Yankee state of Indiana. Her sacrifice was greater than mine.

My mother was in her early forties and the mother of four teenagers when our ministry began to grow extensively and our college and schools started. Dad became increasingly busy at a time when my mother was becoming increasingly busy for a completely different reason. To be honest with you, I don't know how my mother did it.

I thought as a pastor's daughter for 41 years, I understood the stress of being a pastor's wife. Though I did know stress, I did not have a clue to the stresses that my mom and dad endured.

Dedication

I recently read an analogy which reminded me of the temptations to quit that must be a part of the struggle of every pastor's wife. The analogy comes from Psalm 23. The Lord is our shepherd. He uses his rod and staff to comfort us. With His staff, God leads us in His will. With His rod, God chastens us and keeps us in His will.

Sometimes the sheep tire of the pain of the rod and the straight and narrow way by which they are led with God's staff. Though they enjoy the green pastures God provides, sometimes the grass looks greener on the other side. When passing through the valley, some sheep wish to jump the fence when they think the Shepherd is not looking or when He feels far away.

To jump the fence, however, means to leave the protection from the presence of our enemies. The sheep who jumps the fence finds himself vulnerable to the attack of wolves and other predators. The sheep who is found by the seeking Shepherd will be forgiven and given the gift of healing from his kind and loving Shepherd. The Shepherd is willing to leave the fold to go after just one sheep. But oftentimes the sheep is never quite the same as he was before he left the fold.

Having sort of walked in my mother's moccasins for eight years now, I realize not only the countless blessings of being the pastor's wife of a megachurch, but I also realize some of the tensions, stresses, attacks, and heartaches. I know there must have been times when my mother wanted to jump the fence. There must have been times when the grass looked greener and defi-

nitely more private on the other side of the fence. I walked with my mother and father through times when the personal attacks were undeserved, yet almost unbearable for me as their daughter. I see now how much more unbearable they must have seemed for the pastor's wife. Yet Mom remained dedicated to my father's ministry all throughout his life.

Why? Because she loved the people of the First Baptist Church of Hammond, Indiana? Yes, but there must have been more to it than that.

Why? Because she loved her husband? Certainly, but there must have been more to it than that.

Why? Because she loved her children? She was a devoted mother, but there was still more to it than that.

There could only be one reason why a private woman would be faithful to such a public life during times of slander and great stress, as well as during many blessed times. There could be only one reason that would cause my mother to help her husband to finish his race.

Why? The answer is that my mother loved the Great Shepherd. She had a consistent walk with Him, and she was completely dedicated to doing His will in His pasture. If my mother ever longed for another pasture, she never jumped pasture, and for this all who feed today in the pasture of the great First Baptist Church of Hammond, Indiana, owe Mom a great debt. For this reason, I owe my mother a great debt. For this I am truly thankful!

On Being and Staying Committed...

Start by being faithful in the small things.

Do not be surprised when trials come.

Commitment does not mean no more fun.

Know you can only serve one Master.

— Beverly Hyles

One of the last formal portraits of my parents,
Dr. and Mrs. Jack Hyles

7

Southern Grace
Is Reproducing Yourself

*T*here is an old saying that goes something like this: "Don't criticize your neighbor until you have walked a mile in his moccasins." For the past 8 years, I have had the privilege to walk somewhat in the moccasins of my mother, Mrs. Beverly Hyles.

I am often asked how I am doing as the pastor's wife. I usually respond with "Good" or "Great." I am doing good and great. I have a wonderful God, a wonderful husband, and a wonderful family and church.

Would I like to change my lot in life? No way! I knew two things when the pulpit committee called my husband to candidate at our church. First of all, I knew that God had opened a door, and secondly, I knew my husband and I had to walk through it. God's will, as always, is full of wonderful blessings, but in spite of the awkwardness, the greatest blessing of all is to walk in my mother's moccasins. No, I do not enjoy "taking" her position, and no one could ever take her place. But I enjoy knowing her and understanding her better.

I was so thrilled to be able to write my dad's biography. I remember being afraid that he would die before I finished it. I remember laughing at myself and thinking, "That's silly; Dad is not going to die for a long time." Though Dad did not live very much longer, he did live to read his biography.

I thought so many times as I wrote that book, "I wish every person could research and write a book about his mother and father."

I also wish that every person could walk in her mother's moccasins as I have walked. What I have seen has been amazing. There are many things that I could share with you, but what I wish to share with you now is my view of my mother's faithfulness and commitment.

I see from my mother's moccasins that the stress level of the pastor of such a large ministry is overwhelming. Even with a good-spirited husband such as mine, much of this stress is sprinkled down upon the pastor's wife. I do not want you to feel sorry for me or my mother. God's grace is sufficient, and God's people are wonderful. I just want you to look with me for a moment, inside these moccasins, at how amazing it is to practice such a feat for 41 years.

I want to be loved as the pastor's wife. I love to be loved. But I really do not want people to admire me as they have admired my mother. For I have only just put on the shoes that she wore for 41 years. If I have a time to be admired, it will be when I finish my course, take off these moccasins, and hand them to some fortunate lady.

I have not yet walked in the moccasins my mother now

wears. I have not lost my husband of 55 years or my position of 41 years. I do try now to imagine what those moccasins must feel like and to prepare myself for the day when I might wear them. But I can only imagine—I do not know what it is like.

But I do know, only to some degree, what it is like to walk in the moccasins in which my mother walked. In these moccasins I feel very blessed; I feel very fortunate, but most of all, I feel very thankful for her commitment to Christ and the faithfulness to her husband of a woman I call my mother and whom I will always call my pastor's wife.

In closing, allow me to exhort you regarding a statement I am learning very well: "Don't criticize your neighbor until you have walked a mile—maybe many miles—in his moccasins."

On Staying Positive...

Deepen your private devotional life,
especially in the Psalms.

Realize the importance of faithfully
attending the church services.

Realize the importance of listening to your pastor.
"He that is mastered by Christ
is master of every circumstance."

Hear the birds instead of sirens.

Hear laughter instead of complaining.

— Beverly Hyles

Southern Grace
& Charm

Beverly Hyles, 2003

8

Southern Grace
Is Being
a Woman of Lovely Appearance

Very few people who know my mother would describe her without mentioning her beauty. Of course, this beauty is attributed to what God has given her; Beverly Hyles was born with physical beauty, and this was apparent throughout her teen and young adult years. Added to her natural loveliness, Beverly Hyles has done many right things throughout her life to portray and to maintain a beautiful appearance.

As she approaches her eightieth birthday, I can honestly say that Mom is as beautiful and striking as ever, perhaps even more so! She is slimmer and a little blonder (I don't think she will mind my saying that!) than she was in her sixties and early seventies. She is **as** beautiful and I think **more** beautiful than ever. This is a rarity for a woman approaching her eightieth birthday.

Mom has always been striking—a show stopper! I recall shopping with my mother as a teenager and noticing men notice my mother. This was sometimes an egobuster for me. As a teenage girl, I was hoping the teenage boys would be noticing me. Instead, I noticed the men admiring my mother's beauty. My mom was always kind, yet appropriate, and humble in her response to these men.

The most accurate way to describe my mother's beauty is to say that she looks just like a pastor's wife. Even more accurately, my mother looks like a Christian—a daughter of a king—the King. Just how does my mother set these examples in her appearance?

On Why Ladies Should Strive to Look Nice...

People watch you more than you want them to.

You can be an example to others.

Your church wants to be proud of you.

— Beverly Hyles

1. My mother is beautiful in her appearance. God is the Author of all things beautiful, and He obviously enjoys beauty. The world which God created is full of beauty, which varies greatly in color, texture, and style.

When God described the virtuous woman, He described a woman whose *"...clothing is silk and purple."* (Proverbs 31:22) The woman God chose as a pattern woman wore bold colors and elegant fabrics. She was beautiful in her dress.

Proverbs 31:22, *"She maketh herself coverings of tapestry; her clothing is silk and purple."*

When God described the temple and the garments of its priests, He described great elegance and beauty.

In I Corinthians 6:19, God says that we as Christians are now the temples of the Holy Spirit.

I Corinthians 6:19, *"What? know ye not that your body is the temple of the Holy Ghost which is in you, which ye have of God, and ye are not your own?"* This verse illustrates how beautiful God wants us to be in our appearance.

Mom is a woman of good taste. In her book *What Is Modesty?*, Michelle Brock said, "The more like God we become, the more we will be able to evaluate true beauty." Beverly Hyles' godliness helped to portray true beauty.

Mom has always been beautiful in her stature, her figure, her hair, and her wardrobe. I would describe her taste in clothing as classic, yet bright and cheerful. A tailored suit most typifies my mother's style. Yet her suits were never mannish, but they possessed a feminine flair.

2. **My mother is modest in her appearance.** The Bible says that a woman is to be *modest* in her apparel. I Timothy 2:9, *"In like manner also, that women adorn themselves in modest apparel, with shamefacedness and sobriety; not with broided hair, or gold, or pearls, or costly array."* This Bible word *modest* means "to be humble, pure, and appropri-

On Why Ladies Should Strive to Look Nice...

&

You are a daughter of the King.

&

You will have more confidence.

&

Your husband wants to be proud of the way you look.

– Beverly Hyles

ate." It also means "to arrange your wardrobe in such a way so that no one thing is disorderly or no one thing stands out." A woman who dresses modestly presents a whole package which reflects not only a beautiful woman, but also a lovely countenance which reflects a beautiful spirit. Beverly Hyles' wardrobe and appearance could not be described anymore accurately than with the Bible word *modest*.

On Proverbs 7...

God did not put Proverbs 7 in the Bible as an afterthought. God included that chapter as a warning to men, but the chapter is also for women to take responsibility for men's thoughts. It is time for women to set some rules for dress. It is time to decide in our hearts what we believe.

– Beverly Hyles

• My mother is humble and pure in her appearance. Though it is the norm for Mom to wear unique outfits with eye-catching colors and patterns, you never see my mother in anything that I would call gaudy. *Worldliness* is not a word to portray my mother's taste in dress. Neither are the words "out-of-style." *Timeless* would be a more accurate word.

Nothing about my mother's dress has ever drawn a man's attention to anything but her countenance. I once heard a famous evangelist's wife, Cathy Rice, say, "A woman should wear her clothing tight enough to show she is a woman, and loose enough to show she is a lady." My mother never followed the pattern of the Christian who dressed dowdy, drab, and out-of-date. Her clothing has always been perfectly tailored and never ill-fitting. Yet her consistency in dress standards has proven that she is a lady.

Mom did not follow anyone else's dress standards. When mini-skirts were in fashion, she chose to wear her dresses just below her knee. When midi-skirts (mid-calf length) and maxi-skirts (ankle length) were in fashion, she still chose to keep her just-below-the-knee skirt length standard. When sandals have been in fashion, Mom has kept her preference for pumps or closed-toe shoes. She has never preached her standards or preferences as something that everyone else must follow. She has simply set her own classic standard. My mother's hair has never been cut to a manly length or style. She has worn makeup, but it has always been a minimum amount.

On Maintaining Your Outward Appearance…

The greatest beauty treatment for the outward appearance is spending time with God.

— Beverly Hyles

Beverly Hyles has kept the rules that I have been taught portray modesty for a Christian lady.

- ❈ Her clothing is not too tight.
- ❈ Her necklines are never too low.
- ❈ Her fabrics are never too sheer.
- ❈ Her skirts are never too short.

- Her clothing is never too mannish. I do not believe my mother has ever worn a pair of pants.

Yet I have not seen my mother's appearance ridiculed. Why? Because she dresses and cares for herself in such a way that even the world cannot help but respond with a big "WOW!"

- My mother is orderly in her appearance. I Corinthians 14:40 says, *"Let all things be done decently and in order."* The appearance of Beverly Hyles parallels this verse. Her hair is never out of place, and her makeup is neatly arranged. Her wardrobe and entire look are that of overall organization and beauty. I am not saying a lady must have every hair in place at all times to please the Lord in her appearance, but there is never a time for a woman to be unkempt in her looks. The "grunge" look and the "I-just-got-out-of-bed" hairstyles on both men and women do not fit well with God's command in I Corinthians 14:40. My mother is a good role model to follow for an example of what pleases the Lord regarding the orderliness of the appearance of a Christian lady.

On Your Dress...

Your clothes say something about your heart.

— *Beverly Hyles*

- My mother is appropriate in her appearance. I have known Christian women to wear their Sunday suit to a picnic in order to demonstrate their modesty in dress. Though Mom always looked nice even when cleaning the house, she has been appropriate in her dress. I have always been proud of her, and I have never been embarrassed by her appearance.

My mom's casual look most often consists of a casual skirt, perhaps but rarely denim, and a classic-style shirt with an up-to-date color or pattern in the fabric. My sisters and I have said that Mom always looks "fresh." We even teased her about it as teenage girls, but this is something we have tried to emulate as adult ladies.

On Dressing Appropriately…

There are no unimportant days or moments— always dress appropriately.

– Beverly Hyles

• My mother is submissive and humble in her appearance. Mom taught me that the average woman dresses to please people in the following order: first, other women; secondly, herself; and lastly, her husband. Mom said a wise woman will make it her goal to dress to please people in the following order: first, her husband; secondly, herself; and lastly, other women.

The "What-will-the-other-women-think-of-my-dress?" attitude is a proud rather than a humble attitude about dress. It also causes us to neglect the primary people we should be trying to please in our dress: God and our husbands or fathers, depending on whether or not we are married.

To summarize my mother's appearance, I must say this: Beverly Hyles understands her role of bringing both beauty and femininity to everything she wears, as well as to everything she does to herself. The beauty of Mom's physical appearance is truly a beauty of holiness.

Comments From a Southern Belle

When Mrs. Hyles was asked to comment about appearance, she stated the following: "Proper appearance is an attitude. A Christian woman's attitude should be that she is a daughter of the King, and she should dress and care for her appearance in such a manner." Psalm 45:13, *"The king's daughter is all glorious within: her clothing is of wrought gold."*

On My Husband's List for Dressing Appropriately

Always dress at home to be presentable to visitors.

Do not dress in a trendy fashion, but be stylish. Never dress gaudy.

Always dress to the occasion.

Have a clothes budget.

Always dress within your means.

Dress like a modest Christian wife.

Buy for the next year at this year's end-of-season sales.

Dress like your husband wants, even if it is not your preference.

Always appreciate what your husband buys!

— Beverly Hyles

9

Southern Grace
Is Being a Woman
of Disciplined Physical Habits

*W*hen I think of my mother, I cannot help but think of someone who is disciplined in caring for her physical health. I don't think Mom has ever been on a diet, yet she has remained trim all of her life. Her philosophy has been to lose as soon as she puts on a couple of pounds. She does it the old-fashioned way—by cutting back on the number of calories consumed. Because of this, I believe that Beverly Hyles has maintained a healthy metabolism.

In the book *The Schwarzbein Principle* by Dr. Diana Schwarzbein, five tenets are shared for creating a healthy metabolism. Her philosophy is that a person who has a healthy metabolism will naturally arrive and stay at his or her ideal weight. Her tenets target diet, exercise, rest, the avoidance of chemicals, and the proper handling of stress. In this chapter allow me to link those concepts to my mother's life.

Diet

My mother is a person who enjoys eating. My siblings and I have even teased her about this fact. Ecclesiastes 2:24, *"There is nothing better for a man, than that he should eat and drink, and that he should make his soul enjoy good in his labour. This also I saw, that it was from the hand of God."*

Mom prepared and ate a hearty breakfast each morning. She was a three-meal-a-day person, and each meal was not only delicious, but also well-balanced. Mom was also known to snack once or twice a day. Mom's obvious enjoyment of simple things was manifested when she was seen eating.

Philippians 4:5, *"Let your moderation* (self-control) *be known unto all men. The Lord is at hand."* "Moderation," " self-control," and "balance" are all words that describe Beverly Hyles' diet, her physical habits, and all of her life.

Mom has cooked healthy, balanced meals, and she weighs herself regularly. When her weight has risen, she simply has cut back on her portions.

On Dieting…

&

A lifetime of proper eating and exercise is the best diet.

— *Beverly Hyles*

In Chapter 13, I touch on the subject of my mother's cooking. Mom was a great cook. Every evening meal consisted of a main dish with protein, a salad, a vegetable, and sometimes even bread. I am most grateful to my mother for her teaching her children to love vegetables. Mom cooked many vegetables that my Yankee husband had never even heard of, and she made them all taste great! I like to say that my mother could make vegetables sing! They were so flavorful that my husband usually enjoyed any vegetable she prepared with the first try.

This may seem like a minute detail to appreciate about one's parent, but my love for all foods healthy, particularly all kinds of vegetables has made it easy for me to keep my own weight under control. I, like my mother, love to eat. I say that "I never met a food I didn't like!" However, I am just as content to fill my plate with the variety of vegetables and healthy foods that I have learned to love since childhood, as I am to fill it with desserts.

On Dieting...

Our bodies are called the temple of the Holy Spirit; overeating is a sin against the body.

— *Beverly Hyles*

Our home where I grew up also contained in its cupboards some snack foods and desserts. Again, "moderation" was the key word in our family's diet. Snacks and desserts were provided in moderation but were not much of a temptation because our family members were usually filled up on healthy meals.

Exercise

A lifetime of moderate exercise is another way to maintain a healthy metabolism. I have never known my mother to "sweat to the oldies." Mom never manifested a mid-life crisis by training for a marathon. She never joined a health club. Over exercising has been proven to destroy one's metabolism just as much as under eating does. Mom did, however, do calisthenics when she noticed an extra bit of flab here and there. Also my mom worked hard, and she burned a lot of calories that way. As my mother approaches her eightieth birthday, she still has a regular habit of brisk walking. At an age when many women cannot climb stairs, Mom walks a walking track on a regular basis.

I realize that a person's health is a gift from God. All good things do come from Him and are under His control. A woman can discipline herself as Mom has and still suffer from ill health. Yet I notice more and more in my counseling how many American women, who come to me asking for help with issues of fatigue and chronic illness, also confess a lifetime of practicing poor physical habits.

A love for the outdoors has also been a part of Beverly Hyles' exercise regimen. Mom still walks outside whenever an opportunity arises. Flowers and my mother go together like peanut butter goes with jelly. Beauty and Beverly Hyles go together just like a hand and glove.

For 41 years, Mom and Dad lived in the same house in Munster, Indiana. I was brought to that home from the hospital and stayed in that same house until I was married. All of the years my mother lived in that house, the large corner lot was manicured. Though Mom did not mow the lawn, she trimmed the many bushes, and she planted and maintained the flowers. I believe this is another reason that my mother has stayed in such excellent physical shape. It is also an aspect of my mother's life that adds to her charm and femininity.

I occasionally drive past the home where my parents lived for so many years. Now that it has new owners, the yard no longer projects the care it once did when my mother was its caretaker. Mom had a way of working hard to bring beauty to everything she touched. Her effort to bring beauty to her yard and flowers also has helped to keep her in great physical shape.

Rest

Human beings need eight hours of rest a night in order to maintain a proper metabolism. Beverly Hyles has always been a lady who has kept rest in its proper priority. If she did not get eight hours of sleep a night, she has kept it close to that average all of her lifetime. My mother has also been one to take a daily nap. She had a practice of lying on top of the covers in a diagonal position with her hand covering her eyes. (Even her sleep position was consistent, something about which my sisters and I enjoyed teasing her.) Always the dis-

On Keeping the Right Spirit...

❧

When you are not in the right spirit:

❧

It hinders your home.

❧

It hinders your husband.

❧

It hinders your children.

❧

It hinders your health.

❧

It hinders your soul winning.

– Beverly Hyles

ciplined person, her nap was at approximately the same time every day. Mrs. Hyles is well-known and well-beloved for saying frequently, "Sometimes the most spiritual thing you can do is take a nap." Perhaps that statement does not sound very spiritual, but it sure seemed spiritual to me when I arrived home from school. Mom rarely, if ever, greeted me with the fatigued spirit of a "wet dish rag." Instead, she was looking, acting, and seeming to be feeling sharp. The orderliness of our home spoke to me that my mother had been working hard all day, but her emphasis on proper rest emphasized to me this philosophy: it is not so important how fast we go in this life, but rather how long we last.

Avoidance of Chemicals

My mother has been balanced in her approach to medicine. Mom has never been one to resist going to the doctor when she needed to; yet she has not run to the doctor for every little ailment. Mom is not just one who practices good health habits; she is also one who enjoys good health. She reminds me of the virtuous woman about whom it says in Proverbs 31:17, *"She girdeth her loins with strength, and strengtheneth her arms."*

Mom has been careful to avoid the use of chemicals in her life, even if they come in the form of prescription drugs.

A few years ago my mother was diagnosed with a very mild form of osteoporosis. The doctor recommended a drug to treat the disease. Rather than taking the drug, Mom tried several natural cures. Her doctor has since diagnosed her disease to be in remission. This is just typical of Mom's moderate ideals and practices about medicine and chemicals.

Mom has also been good to study the use of natural supplements as health aids and has used them consistently and in moderation. I believe consistent study of and using of natural supplements has helped my mother to avoid a need for chemical drugs.

Stress

All of life contains stress. John 16:33 says, *"...In the world ye shall have tribulation...."* Yet the individual's handling of stress can vary greatly from one person to another. Poor handling of stress is another tenet by which one's metabolism can be thrown off balance. Stress can cause a person to run out of energy for exercise. It can also cause a person to eat for comfort, to suffer from insomnia, and to find a retreat in drugs such as antidepressants. For these reasons, as well as what poor handling of stress can do to a person's overall health, a proper approach to stress is of utmost importance to a person's physical habits.

I would like to share with you some of my mom's pointers on minimizing stress from one of her own outlines that she taught in her college classes.

On Staying on Top...

1. Don't spend too much time with negative people.
2. If you must spend time with a negative person, plan your conversation ahead of time. *(continued)*

3. Look for someone who needs your help.
4. Sing and listen to happy songs.
5. Shield yourself from negatives in magazines, radio, news reports, etc.
6. Don't spend time talking about your problems to everyone you meet.
7. Don't bring your problems home. Make home a peaceful, restful place.
8. Be alert for people who need you.
9. Have optimistic people you can talk to if you need to talk.
10. Talk about your problems only when seeking counsel.
11. Plan a scheduled time to think about your problems.
12. Plan good thoughts to counteract the negative.
13. Never miss church.
14. Develop a hobby that demands your attention.
15. Have something to look forward to every day.
16. Plan mini-vacations.
17. Schedule your Bible and prayer time—your time alone with God.
18. Schedule regular dates with your husband.
19. Get plenty of rest and take care of your health.
20. Learn to be thankful and praise God in everything. I Thessalonians 5:18, *"In every thing give thanks: for this is the will of God in Christ Jesus concerning you."* Philippians 2:13, *"For it is God which worketh in you both to will and to do of his good pleasure."*

— *Beverly Hyles*

At least weekly, I pray and ask God to help me to be a helper to my husband spiritually, in his ministry, and physically. When I ask God to allow me to help my husband physically, I am asking for wisdom to give him proper counsel regarding illnesses, medicines, rest, exercise, and so forth. Most of the physical healthcare does, after all, rest in the hands of the wife and mother. Much of whatever wisdom God has given me regarding these areas has come from my moth-

On Being the Wife of the Leader...

&

The main job of the leader's wife is to be the leader's wife.

– Beverly Hyles

er. She truly has been a help meet to her family in the area of physical habits.

As I have already mentioned, in 2008 my mother was diagnosed with Phase I, Stage I breast cancer. Her cancer was removed, and Mom went through six weeks of radiation treatments. Chemotherapy was not deemed necessary by her doctor. Mom's doctor prescribed a chemical prescription hormone blocker, which my mom opted not to take. She is instead pursuing natural methods. One of the most difficult things for me regarding my mother's fight with cancer has been seeing her lose a bit of her good health, which she has guarded so diligently.

I predict that my mother will have many years of good health ahead. My prayer is that she will live to be at least as old as her mother did, which was 95 years of age. Whenever and however God calls my mother to Heaven and should she precede me to Heaven, I will have the peace of knowing that my mom took the best care of her health as she knew how. I am thankful for a mother who is moderate in her approach to physical habits.

---

[1]Beverly Hyles, "The Wife of the Leader" (unpublished class notes, Hyles-Anderson College, 1995).

10

Southern Grace
Is Being a Feminine Lady

*I*f there is any comment that has been frequently made about Beverly Hyles, it is this: "Beverly Hyles is the epitome of a lady. She is the essence of femininity."

Many people feel that femininity comes from without. It is judged first by many in the way a woman stands, sits, dresses, and so forth. I think not! Femininity is first an inward attitude. The inward attitude of a true lady will almost naturally manifest femininity in the outward choices and actions of that lady.

I believe that my mother's femininity starts from the inside. First of all, because Mom has always understood that her role is completely opposite from a man, she is content in that role. Mom is comfortable in her femininity, and she has great respect for the importance of the role of what I would call the "traditional woman."

I have written in other chapters about the great strength and dedication that Beverly Hyles has practiced in her life. Mom is of the realization that being a true lady in a traditional role is not for sissies. It takes great strength to be a true lady, and being a

On Femininity…

If we are not
feminine…

We rob God of His
perfect plan for us.

We rob other ladies of
the inspiration
and gracious example
we can be.

We rob men of
the opportunity
to show their
masculinity.

We rob ourselves of
the beauty that comes
only by conforming to
His divine will.

— Beverly Hyles

true lady in no way means being a weak lady.

Secondly, my mother's femininity comes from the inside because of her own belief in herself. Mom has studied many books on the subject of self-esteem. She realizes the value of having proper self-esteem. I don't believe that gaining an appropriate sense of self-esteem has come naturally for Beverly Hyles.

The very position of being the pastor's wife of a megachurch can destroy self-esteem. So many people observe you, and there are so many expectations that a pastor's wife is prone to put upon herself. I believe my mother's lifestyle and her struggle with self-esteem prompted her not only to thoroughly study the subject of self-esteem but also to teach the subject to other ladies. Her desire has been to help other ladies in the area where she has struggled.

Mom has encouraged me personally in the area of self-esteem, and she has recommended good reading to me through the years on this very important subject. Growing up in the limelight and being a rather absentminded youngest child, I needed this emphasis in my life. Self-esteem has not been something which has come naturally to me either, and I am thankful for the direction Mom pointed me in during my struggles as a teenager.

Mom has written one book and a booklet on the subject of self-esteem which have been bestsellers and continue to be well-beloved to this day. They are entitled, *I Feel Precious to God* and *You Are Somebody!* Even the titles of these books betray that my mother's self-esteem comes from God and not from a career.

Thirdly, my mother's femininity comes from within herself because of her desire to serve. My mother has served in many capacities throughout her life, but her domestic service stands out in my mind as one of her most feminine accomplishments. Beverly Hyles has always loved domestic duties. She has always given them great priority in her life, and that in itself caused her to be somewhat the servant of our home. Yet she exalted this position, and her

On Being Gracious Toward Other Ladies…

Receiving God's love personally, knowing that you are cherished by Him will help dispel envy or comparison.

To become very familiar with Psalm 139 is a great source of confidence in who we are because of Whose we are.

— *Beverly Hyles*

service only added to her femininity and her strength.

Understanding and believing in her role, having proper self-esteem, and loving domestic service have all combined themselves to create a feminine attitude in Beverly Hyles—the essence of femininity. Mom's feminine attitude clearly manifests itself in her outward behavior.

On Gracious Speech…

There is such power in words. We have the ability every day to build or tear down everyone we meet. A good rule is found in James 1:19, *"…to be swift to hear, slow to speak, slow to anger."*

We don't have to have the last word. In His persecution, Jesus answered not a word!

— Beverly Hyles

1. Beverly Hyles is feminine in her speech. I have dedicated an entire chapter on my mother's speech, but at this point, I want to mention her Southern drawl and the pleasant softness of her voice. Mom has always been known to have a quiet spirit.

I Peter 3:4, *"But let it be the hidden man of the heart, in that which is not corruptible, even the ornament of a meek and quiet spirit, which is in the sight of God of great price."* This verse magnifies inward femininity and a quiet spirit.

Mom has never been one to be loud in the volume of her voice. I am not implying that there is never a time to talk or cheer loudly, but we can all learn from my mother. A person who is yelling at the referee at her son's ball game certainly is not displaying a quiet spirit. There has never been a time when I have heard my mother yell publicly or talk in such a manner as to draw attention to herself individually.

Beverly Hyles lived in Texas for the first 30 years of her life. Though she spent the next 43 years of her life in Indiana, she never lost her Southern drawl. We cannot all copy my mother's drawl, nor should we, but the charming speech of my mom could not be properly portrayed without mentioning her Southern drawl.

2. Beverly Hyles is feminine in her appearance. Again, an entire chapter has been devoted to my mother's appearance, but it had to be mentioned in connection with Mom's femininity. My mother has never worn pants. Perhaps the most divisive issue among Christians today would be the issue of women's wearing of pants. The purpose of this book is not to settle this issue but rather to illuminate the qualities of my mother which I believe set her apart.

Deuteronomy 22:5 says, *"The woman shall not wear that which per-taineth unto a man, neither shall a man put on a woman's garment: for all that do so are abomination unto the LORD thy God."* Even though this verse is an Old Testament command, we know that it is relevant for today by the words *"abomination unto the LORD thy God."* The Old Testament laws which the Bible states are an "abomination to man" are obviously very changeable. Yet God changes not, so that which He hated in the Old Testament, He still hates today.

When I occasionally see a man dressed in a skirt or wearing makeup, I feel unsettled. Why? Deuteronomy does not tell me that a skirt or pants is the issue. Yet seeing a man in clothing which pertains to a woman causes me to fear the loss of the traditional separation of the genders.

You may not agree with Beverly Hyles' choice to wear only dresses and skirts, but you must admit that in doing so she is helping to pass on a high standard for the separation of men and women. Genesis 1:27, *"So God created man in his own image, in the image of God created he him; male and female created he them."*

I was not allowed to wear pants as a little girl growing up in my parents' home, at a time when they were becoming more popular. School dress codes were greatly loosened and for the most part ceased to exist when I was attending elementary school. Many of the girls at the public school that I attended through the fifth grade wore dresses to class. Yet they were all required to wear pants to gym class. My parents, however, made an agreement with the teacher that I would wear a skirt. I was embarrassed, so I sneaked a pair of snow pants to gym class one day. During that class, the zipper broke on my snow pants, and I have never worn pants since.

During my twenties, I struggled with my decision about pants. I regret to say that I was tired of looking different in public. I came to a turning point in my struggle when I made my final decision that I would value my mom and dad more than an item made of fabric called a pair of pants. I would honor my father's wishes and my mother's example. My father went to Heaven eight years ago, and silly as it may seem, that decision has held great significance in my life since his death, and I have been thankful over and over for the choice I have made.

As I write about my mother and her femininity, I am again grateful for that choice. I wish to do for my children and grandchildren what my mom did for me. I wish to pass on a high standard for the separation of the genders. I also wish to dress as sharp as my mother. It is hard to disdain my mother's appearance, though she may be seen somewhere as the only woman in a dress. She always looks first-class and beautiful.

3. Beverly Hyles is feminine in her hairstyle. Mom has worn her hair in several lengths and styles, but her hairstyle has always had a softness about it. Her hair has never been severely short, trendy, or what I would call "chopped." Her hairstyle is always that of a lady, and it never speaks as so many modern hairstyles do so as to say, "I don't need a man."

4. Beverly Hyles is feminine in her behavior. Not only is my mother's inward spirit a feminine one, but so is her conversation of life or behavior. Mom stands and walks as a lady. She is tall and trim, which adds to the elegance of her feminine walk. Though she is tall, she does not slouch, but she walks with great pos-

On Being a Charming Lady…

Get organized! Prepare for the day and whom you meet. Don't let life just happen to you; you make life happen.

Make sure you are well-groomed.

Do something regularly for another as a surprise.

Do something every day to make your home a more pleasant place to be.

— *Beverly Hyles*

ture and dignity. Her strides are small and feminine as is the way she carries her head and arms.

My father used to say, "Beverly has a swing in her backyard." His statement does not mean she walks seductively. Rather, all of her movements are graceful and singularly feminine. I am tempted to give a lesson on walk here, but instead I will admonish my readers. Find someone who knows how to walk and ask that person to teach you how. Also, develop an inward attitude of femininity. Then your walk will at least somewhat naturally become the opposite of a man's walk.

My mother sits as a lady, again with great posture. Having never worn pants, it is not difficult for Mom to remember to be feminine when sitting—legs together or crossed at the knees or ankles—hands folded appropriately on her lap. You will never see my mother with her arms crossed, hands under her elbows. I have been taught that this posture is a stubborn posture, which my mother avoids.

5. Beverly Hyles is feminine in her added touches. That by which my mother makes her mark is feminine. Mom is known for always carrying a lace handkerchief, as well as for bright, classy, and modest clothing and shoes. Her purses are one of her trademarks. They are always feminine and unique.

Growing up in her home, I recall Mom's always wearing an apron when she cooked, and it was always clean and feminine.

There was an old television show made in the 1950s called "Leave It to Beaver." It is one of the last shows to have been aired that showed a traditional family. The mother, who was named June Cleaver, on that show was graceful, feminine, domestic, and to be admired.

In the twenty-first century, I have heard women negatively remark, "She is a June Cleaver." Yet just as was shown on the television series "Leave It to Beaver," where there is a graceful, feminine, and domestic wife and mother, there is a traditional and happy family.

Many women did not grow up in a traditional and happy home, and therefore, they do not feel feminine. This chapter is not written to shame anyone or to hurt another's self-esteem. It is written to point a lady to what she could become. It is written to encourage every lady to believe in her femininity once again and to push the reset button for all of us to pass on femininity to our daughters and granddaughters.

Most of all, it is written to thank my mother for giving me an example for passing on the tradition of femininity and to thank her for being the epitome of a lady and the essence of femininity.

On Speech…

Sound speech
"healthy, correct, safe" talk that becomes holiness.

Pure speech
Philippians 4:8

Excellent speech
"Excellent speech becometh not a fool." (Proverbs 17:7a)

Edifying speech—uplifting, building speech

Careful speech
"And whatsoever ye do in word or deed, do all in the name of the Lord Jesus,
giving thanks to God and the Father by him."
(Colossians 3:17)

Healing speech
"Brethren, if a man be overtaken in a fault, ye which are spiritual, restore
such an one in the spirit of meekness…." (Galatians 6:1)

– *Beverly Hyles*

11

Southern Grace
Is Being Appropriate
in Your Manners and Speech

*A*ppropriate and *first-class* would be two terms which would describe Beverly Hyles. My mother is appropriate and first-class in her speech. Mom has not been one to take on slang or crude words as a part of her vocabulary. Mom is feminine in her word choices.

Beverly Hyles is not a gossip. *"A froward man soweth strife: and a whisperer separateth chief friends."* (Proverbs 16:28)

As a pastor's wife, my mom did a lot of counseling. As a young girl living at home, I recall my mother's counseling by way of the telephone. Yet I do not recall Mom's discussing the subject matter of her counseling. The secrets of those whom she counseled were and are safe with her. My mother was not one to use the telephone excessively, nor was she one to socialize much. She often excused herself early from meetings to be at home for her family. All of these helped her reach her goal of resisting gossip.

On Gracious Manners...

Gracious manners begin with "Do unto others as you would have them do unto you." Ephesians 4:32, *"...Be ye kind one to another...."*

– *Beverly Hyles*

Beverly Hyles is not sarcastic. *"As a mad man who casteth firebrands, arrows and death, So is the man that deceiveth his neighbor and saith, Am not I in sport?"* (Proverbs 26:18)

Sarcasm, I must admit, was a favorite pastime in our family when I was growing up. Everyone in our family was sarcastic. We tried not to let our sarcasm cross the line of hurting people, but we were all sarcastic—except for Mom. My mother has a sweet innocence about herself that caused her not just to avoid speaking sarcastically—she really didn't think that way. My mother didn't always participate in humor, but she was oh so fun to play a trick on. Her innocence made it so. Mom's lack of sarcasm is not something to be mocked, but rather something to be admired! It is a sweet innocence that has made her who she is.

Beverly Hyles is not opinionated! She does not speak all of her mind. *"A fool uttereth all his mind: but a wise man keepeth it in till afterwards."* (Proverbs 29:11) Though Mom was very available for her family, she was not one to give her opinions unnecessarily.

When my mother woke me around 2:00 a.m. to tell me, "I just met a young man and his family, and I think you should date this young man," I was startled! Though my father had given me a lot of dating advice through the years, Mom had given me very little. Mom was a quiet presence in our house. When she did give advice, it was pretty reliable. I ended up marrying the one man she advised me to date, and we have lived happily ever after.

Beverly Hyles is not rude or crude in her speech or behavior! Ephesians 4:29, *"Let no corrupt communication proceed out of your mouth, but that which is good to the use of edifying, that it may minister grace unto the hearers."*

I have never heard my mother participate in what is sometimes called "bathroom" or "bedroom" talk. I know that it is said to "never say 'never.' " Nobody "never" does anything! But I believe I can honestly say that my mother is never crude in her behavior or speech.

Beverly Hyles is mannerly in her speech. Her "please" and "thank you's" flow freely, whether it be by way of the spoken word or the written word. My mother and father taught their children to use "sir's" and "ma'am's" frequently, and Mom led by example.

When needed, my mother would approach me with those magic words, "I'm sorry." This is something that I respect my mom for immensely. Her willingness to be real and admit fault has always stood out in my mind when I think about the strengths of my mother.

My siblings and I were taught table manners, and we were not allowed to leave the table without asking, "May I please be excused?" We were taught to answer the telephone with: "Good morning, this is Cindy Hyles." or "Good afternoon, this is Cindy Hyles." or "Good evening, this is Cindy Hyles." One evening I got a little bit flustered and said, "Good night, this is Cindy Hyles!"

We were taught how to shake hands and how to look people in the eye when talking with them. My siblings and I were taught how to answer the door.

Beverly Hyles is mannerly in her behavior, and she taught her children to be so. We were taught matters of personal hygiene, cleanliness and orderliness, whether it was to our person or to our surroundings. These teachings may sound basic and common, but I have learned through my counseling as a pastor's wife that these teachings are unfortunately not so commonplace.

Saturday was a time when Mom shined our shoes and laid out our best clothing. We bathed, washed our hair, and did all of the extras when Saturday evening came, so that we would be at our best for what was always church day—Sunday!

Beverly Hyles is *sweet* in her speech and behavior! Ephesians 4:32, *"And be ye kind one to another, tenderhearted, forgiving one another, even as God for Christ's sake hath forgiven you."*

My father often bragged that in all of his years of ministry and all the different churches and people he pastored, my mom never made an enemy. Everyone loved my mother and her kind and gracious ways. She has a manner which comes across gracious and not abrasive to others.

Beverly Hyles is *truthful* in her speech and behavior! Ephesians 4:25, *"Wherefore putting away lying, speak every man truth to his neighbour: for we are members one of another."*

My generation and the generations following seem not to value truth as my parents' generation has done. Both my mother and father have been truthful and honest in their dealings with all. Their word is as good as their bond.

Beverly Hyles is *appropriate* in her speech and behavior. Proverbs 25:11 *"A word fitly* [or appropriately] *spoken is like apples of gold in pictures of silver."*

My mother's avoidance of crude and rude speech and behavior was mentioned previously. As a pastor's wife for several decades, Mom also learned to speak the appropriate words at the appropriate time. There are many examples of this, but the most shining example of my mother's appropriateness would be the words spoken at my father's funeral. The fact that she had the strength to speak at my dad's funeral at all was amazing. But the appropriateness and the inspiration of her words were even more amazing!

Beverly Hyles is *respectful* in her speech and behavior. Luke 22:32, *"...and when thou art converted, strengthen the brethren."*

Mom has had a way of speaking to men so that she makes them feel masculine and appreciated without being in any way flirtatious or inappropriate. She especially demonstrates this ability in her speech and manner toward authorities.

This is not an etiquette book, but I could fill a book with writing just the many ways that my mother has displayed proper etiquette. This is not a book about gracious speech, but chapter after chapter could be written about the graciousness of Mom's speech. I could never in one chapter fully describe the speech or manners of a woman with true grace. But I hope in some way this chapter has conveyed to you what a first-class and appropriate lady Beverly Hyles has been—both in her manners and in her speech.

Beverly Hyles is gracious in her speech and behavior

toward her enemies. My father was a pastor for over 53 years. Many of those years, he pastored a megachurch. Dad was also a strong preacher; he took a strong stand against sin, and he had high standards and convictions. All of these facts opened up my dad for much criticism. He was one of the most beloved people I knew, and he was one of the most criticized people I knew. Of course, an enemy of my father's was also an enemy of my mother's. When he hurt, she hurt. I admire the way my mother handled her enemies.

1. **My mother stayed out of trouble, as much as possible.** Proverbs 27:15, 16, *"A continual dropping in a very rainy day and a contentious woman are alike.* [16]*Whosoever hideth her* [keeps her out of things] *hideth the wind, and the ointment of his right hand, which bewrayeth itself."*

This is the way that I would most describe Mom's response to troubles in the ministry: she stayed out of it; she was uninvolved. My mom understood and enjoyed her role as a wife and housekeeper, and she used that role to comfort and protect her from negative outside influences. She made our home a refuge, and she used it for a refuge. Mom stayed too busy to get involved

On Forgiveness...

&

An unforgiving heart kills emotionally and physically. It will hurt you more than anything else. Forgiveness is (1) basic to your character, (2) basic to your physical health, and (3) basic to your emotional health.

— *Beverly Hyles*

with enemies.

2. My mother did not defend herself or others. She did not defend my father. She may have spoken positively about my father, but she stayed on the offense; she did not get on the defense. Proverbs 17:28, *"Even a fool, when he holdeth his peace, is counted wise: and he that shutteth his lips is esteemed a man of understanding."*

3. My mother controlled her anger. Proverbs 16:32, *"He that is slow to anger is better than the mighty; and he that ruleth his spirit than he that taketh a city."* Mom did not handle the attacks of enemies by flying off the handle or losing her temper. Beverly Hyles is a woman who displays her strength by being remarkably in control of her emotions.

On Being Gracious to Those Who Hurt Us...

Realize we are commanded to love our enemies and to forgive any who offend.
Forgiveness is a characteristic most like God.
It sets us free from the one who has brought hurt.

— *Beverly Hyles*

4. My mother loved and forgave her enemies. Luke 6:27, 28, 37, *"But I say unto you which hear, Love your enemies, do good to them which hate you, "28 Bless them that curse you, and pray for them which despitefully use you. "37 Judge not, and ye shall not be judged: condemn not, and ye shall not be condemned: forgive, and ye shall be forgiven."*

On Attaining Charm…

Believe in yourself.

Make people feel important.

Really be the woman God wants you to be.
Be encouraging, be nourishing, and be healing.

Having a kind heart helps much in successful living.

Remember you cannot be charming without energy.

Set a goal to achieve; it keeps life interesting.

Don't be cynical; rather, learn to be optimistic.

Express the joy of life; nothing is more attractive than joy.

Happiness comes from happenings. Act as if you have a guest
with you for a whole month. You do—the Holy Spirit.

— *Beverly Hyles*

12

Southern Grace
Is Being a "Gracious Woman Who Retaineth Honor"

For years I have watched my mother, Mrs. Jack Hyles, maintain what I call a "gracious reserve" between herself and members of the opposite gender. Her ability to be gracious and friendly and yet never in any way to be indiscreet has often amazed me, especially because she has always been so beautiful. I have tried to put down in writing just what it means to have a "gracious reserve." Please allow me to share some of these ideas with you.

1. Look a man in the eyes only. Not only should you look a man in the eyes, but you should keep a discreet look in your eye. I still cannot exactly describe what a look of discretion is, but I have seen what it is not. Maybe just being aware of how we are coming across will help a girl to look at a man in the proper way.

2. Maintain a safe distance between yourself and a man with whom you are talking. A safe distance will keep a short girl from looking up at a taller man as if she has just been struck by lightning.

3. Talk to a man in a courteous, but formal tone of voice. There should be a definite difference in the tone of voice a wife uses with her husband and the one she uses with other men.

4. Maintain good posture when talking with other men. I may stand slouchy and "cute" when I am talking to my husband, but I would not want to do that with someone else's husband lest I give a wrong impression.

5. When greeting a married couple, always acknowledge the wife first. Also, when you are conversing with a couple, include the wife in the conversation as much as possible.

6. Never follow a man with your eyes after he has passed you. I have seen some young girls get so excited about passing a married man whom they admire that they practically fall apart emotionally. Surely a lady can learn to make a man feel welcome and respected without causing him (or his wife) to have a cardiac arrest.

7. Never ride alone in a car with a man. I take it a step further and never allow myself to be the only lady in a car full of males, unless my husband is one of them.

8. Never compliment a man about his appearance. One may tell a good male friend in the presence of his wife that she likes his tie. That would be very different from saying, "Wow! You sure look nice today."

9. Other than a handshake, I believe touching members of the opposite sex is unnecessary. (This does not include members of the immediate family.)

10. Of course, suggestive conversation is always inappropriate—even in jest.

11. Shower your preacher with lots of gifts and notes of praise, but include his wife in all your thoughtful deeds. As soon as my husband and I became engaged, I made it a practice never to write a man telling him how much I enjoyed his preaching without also including my fiancé's name on the note.

12. Don't counsel with men about sexual problems. Also be careful about counseling with any man on a regular basis, in a secluded area, or late at night.

13. It is my opinion that it is unwise for a woman to allow someone other than her husband to depend too heavily on her. For example, a secretary should not also be the baby sitter for her boss's children, errand runner for her boss's wife, etc. Tragedy often happens when a secretary becomes like "just another member of the family."

14. Last but not least, sow what you want to reap. Sometimes single girls may be too friendly with married men, thinking they have nothing to lose. However, if the Biblical law of sowing and reaping is accurate,

On Being Gracious With Members of the Opposite Gender…

Starts with making the choice of being the strange woman of Proverbs 7 who was the downfall of men or being the woman described in Proverbs 31.

A pure mind is the most important thing in keeping these relationships on a high plane.

— *Beverly Hyles*

then she has everything to lose. I tell my students at Hyles-Anderson College to "treat other women's husbands the way you want yours to be treated" because that is exactly what will happen.

Proverbs 22:3 says, *"A prudent man forseeth the evil, and hideth himself: but the simple pass on, and are punished."* Let's take advance precautions to prevent disaster in the lives of ourselves, those about whom we care, and God's people.

One more thing—thank you, Mom, for being a "gracious woman who retaineth honor" and also for being graciously reserved. This has revealed to me that you truly are a beautiful lady.

Unit 4

Southern Grace
& Homemaking

Beverly Hyles being a diligent homemaker

13

Southern Grace
Is Being a Diligent Homemaker

*B*everly Hyles was and is the ultimate homemaker. My husband, Dr. Jack Schaap, has said, "Your goal as a homemaker should be to make your home a place of peace and order where your husband can renew himself in body and in spirit." This is what my mother did! Home was not just a place where my father found relaxation; it was a place where all our family found relaxation.

Mom used her home as a refuge. I believe this is what gave her the strength to be gracious as she was in public walking among so many people.

My mother was excellent in her care of her family's clothing. The laundry was never behind. My dad used to say that it seemed we threw our clothes down the laundry chute, and they magically ended up folded neatly in our drawers again. Mom did her duties efficiently and without fanfare.

My mother was organized in her shopping. She purchased her groceries once a week on the same day each week. As I have already mentioned, Mom shopped at the same grocery store for nearly all the years that she lived in Northwest Indiana.

My mother was an immaculate house cleaner. She did a thorough weekly cleaning every Monday. There was a place for everything, and everything was in its place.

My mother was the ultimate cook! Included in this chapter are some of my mom's best recipes.

Mom was Southern in her style of cooking. She can and does make everything taste good; I like to say she makes food sing! Even her vegetables are "singing" with flavor.

On Gracious Homemaking…

As with most things, to be a "keeper at home" is our choice. I Corinthians 14:40, *"Do everything decently and in order."* This includes our daily activities. God never tells us in His Word anything that we cannot do.

– Beverly Hyles

My mother is a first-class decorator. Her taste is traditional and classy.

How has Beverly Hyles achieved success in all these areas as a homemaker?

1. **She had a good example.** My maternal grandmother, Eva Slaughter, was a magnificent cook and a good housekeeper.

2. **She was a stayer at home.** To be a truly effective homemaker, Mom had to spend a lot of time at home.

Money is the number-one reason why women do not stay at home. To be honest, though I never went without, we lived very modestly during my childhood. I had a nice, but simple wardrobe. My father drove a red Plymouth car for awhile that had a hole in the floor.

When Mom and Dad got older, the church had truly spoiled them, and they had met with some financial success. But money was not an issue with them then. Money and doing without were never topics of discussion in our household.

3. She was content. As I stated in the previous point, my mother did not discuss what we did or did not have. It may seem like a contradiction, but contentment and being an effective housekeeper go together. Mom and Dad lived in the same house for almost 40 years. In the last few years of my father's life, he moved with my mother into a condominium, so that Mom could better care for herself in case anything happened to Dad. Up until that time, I had only known my parents to live in one house.

4. She had confidence in her job as a homemaker. I teach my students at Hyles-Anderson College

On Homemaking…

❦

Set a goal
to be prepared.

❦

Stay on track!
Things get out of
order so easily.

❦

Don't forget
the small details.

❦

Do everything
to the best of your
ability.
Ecclesiastes 9:10a,
*"Whatsoever thy hand
findeth to do,
do it with thy might."*

— *Beverly Hyles*

that "the key to doing anything efficiently is to like what you are doing." Beverly Hyles truly loved her role and was comfortable being a housewife. I believe this makes Mom a Proverbs 31 woman. Proverbs 31 teaches us that the virtuous woman was focused principally on her household.

Proverbs 31:15, *"She riseth also while it is yet night, and giveth meat to her household…."*

Proverbs 31:21, *"She is not afraid of the snow for her household: for all her household are clothed with scarlet."*

Proverbs 31:27, *"She looketh well to the ways of her household…."*

It is not wrong to have an outside job. Proverbs 31 seems to teach that the virtuous woman had a personal source for creating income. Yet I believe the centerpiece of a woman's mindset should be her household.

5. She accepted the fact that her husband would be the one who was well-known outside of the household. Proverbs 31:23, *"Her husband is known in the gates, when he sitteth among the elders of the land."*

Beverly Hyles became well-known, but it was not because she was climbing the corporate ladder. She was helping someone else to climb his ladder, and she found herself at the top with him. Mom always seemed quite surprised to find herself at the top of anything, a characteristic which I find quite charming in her.

6. She did not expect her husband to share in the household responsibilities. Mom taught herself to do as much of the work around the house as she could. She did not expect the domestic duties to be a 50/50 proposition. When Dad became more financially stable, he was able to pay for just about anything to be done in the house that was needed. When my father was younger, he was not a "Mr. Fix-it" kind of guy. Dad was always eager to please, and he did what he could for my mother, but home for my dad seemed to be a place where he could relax. Well, home should have been a place where Dad could relax. I think, though, that it was more a place where he took what little time that he had and used it to clown around with and to express his love for his family. It was my mother, however, who made much of that possible.

7. **She developed outside interests which brought her closer to her husband and his ministry.** Mom's outside interests did not compete with her job as a homemaker.

8. **She simplified the job of housekeeping.** I learned four things from my mother that have helped me to simplify my job. Just because something is done first-class does not mean that it must be done in a complicated manner.

- Don't buy things you don't need.
- Get rid of things you don't use. Don't hoard things.
- Use calendars and lists.
- Create a simple schedule and live by it strictly.

9. **She put great emphasis on atmosphere.** I don't know if Mom realized what she was doing, but in homemaking, she appealed to all five senses in a great way. She appealed to sight with beautiful and seasonal decorations. (Mom also loved her fireplace.) She appealed to sound with lovely music. I recall the daily radio programs that Mom played consistently and the beautiful music that she played. She appealed to taste by her amazing cooking and baking. She appealed to smell not only

through delicious food, but also through scented candles. She appealed to touch in a myriad of ways, through her own hugs and in her homemaking.

I was perhaps the messiest of all four of my mother's children. During high school and college, my bedroom sometimes looked like World War III had been fought in it. But when I became a wife, I realized that I had learned much by Mom's example.

- I do a load or two of laundry a day and rarely fall behind.
- I grocery shop once a week on the same day and at the same store.
- I cleaned my house every Monday for the first 25 years of my marriage. (Mom has said if her funeral is on my house cleaning day, she fears I won't come.)
- I love to cook and bake for my family, and I make a large Sunday dinner for them every week, as my mother used to do.
- I love to decorate seasonally, for holidays and just in general. I enjoy bringing beauty to my outdoor and indoor environment. I love, love, love, love, love flowers.
- I love clocks, calendars, and lists.
- I get rid of things I don't use. My husband has said he is grateful I have not thrown him away when I am doing spring cleaning.
- I absolutely adore the job of homemaking, and I still feel like I am playing house when I take care of my home and husband.
- I created a simple schedule, and I live by it strictly.

- I use my house very much for a refuge for my husband and me.

I am not trying to brag on myself; I am just saying that *I have become my mother.* Well, I guess that might be bragging. I am not even a fraction of the lady my mother is, but I have learned more than I ever thought I would, perhaps more than she ever thought I would, from her example. I am trying to emphasize the importance of setting a good example for our daughter and the daughters of others in the area of homemaking. If your daughter becomes you, what kind of a lady, what kind of a homemaker will she be?

I rarely counseled with my mother about my marriage. But one time, as a very young wife, I called her with a marriage problem. The problem was pretty much mine rather than my husband's.

Mom's advice was this: why don't you go fix your husband's favorite meal and make his favorite dessert? Be sure the house is clean and that you look lovely when he comes home. Light some candles and create a lovely atmosphere. Then welcome him home with a big kiss and hug.

I got off the phone and thought, "What does that have to do with anything?"

Now at 49, I realize that creative homemaking has almost everything to do with everything. Many, maybe most, women have forgotten that. I am thankful that my mother did not!

Some Favorite Recipes of Beverly Hyles

Strawberry Punch

> 2 envelopes strawberry Kool-Aid
>
> 2 cups sugar
>
> 2 quarts water
>
> 2 cups pineapple juice
>
> 1 quart ginger ale
>
> 1 pint strawberries, crushed

Mix all ingredients and chill.

Southern Sweet Tea

> 7 tea bags
>
> 3 slices lemon (optional)
>
> 8 cups boiling water
>
> 2 cups sugar
>
> 8 cups cold water

Steep the bags in boiling water for 10 minutes. Remove bags, add sugar and lemon while hot. Stir well. Add cold water. (Add ice when ready to serve.)

> (From *Aunt Bee's Mayberry Cookbook*)

Meringue Kisses

    1 egg white
    1 cup nut meats
    1 cup brown sugar, not packed

Preheat oven to 325°. Beat egg whites stiff. Add brown sugar and nuts. Drop by teaspoonfuls on sprayed (Pam) cookie sheet. Turn oven off. Leave in oven 2 or 3 hours or overnight.

Chess Pie

    1 unbaked 9-inch pie shell
    ½ cup butter, melted
    1½ cups sugar
    1½ teaspoons cornmeal
    1½ teaspoons vinegar
    3 eggs

Preheat oven to 450°. Combine butter and sugar. Add cornmeal, vinegar, and eggs. Mix on low speed. Pour into pie shell. Immediately reduce heat to 400° for 15 minutes then reduce heat to 300° and bake for 20-30 minutes. The filling will puff up, so give the pie a jiggle to be sure the center is firm before removing from the oven.

Pistachio Pudding

Crust:

> 1 cup flour
>
> 1 cup walnuts
>
> 2 sticks margarine

Filling:

> 1 8-ounce cream cheese
>
> 1 8-ounce container Cool Whip
>
> 1 cup confectioners' sugar
>
> 4 cups milk
>
> 1 small package pistachio pudding*
>
> Nuts

Mix crust ingredients and press into pan, 9x13 inches. Bake at 350° for 15 minutes.

Mix cream cheese, 1 cup Cool Whip, and sugar together. Put on top of crust. Mix pudding and milk. Pour over mixture. When pudding has set up, top with remaining Cool Whip and nuts.

*You can use chocolate pudding, too!

Sunday Dinner

1-3 pounds rump roast

1 onion

4-5 potatoes

3-4 carrots

2-3 pounds fresh green beans

Bacon grease or vegetable oil

1 pound package frozen broccoli

1 pound package frozen cauliflower

Velveeta cheese, melted

Generously rub roast with salt and pepper. Brown roast at high heat in oven. When brown, add onion, potatoes, carrots around roast. Add 1½ cups water. Cover roasting pan tightly. Cook at 350° until you leave for church. Reduce heat to 250° and cook until you return. Prepare snapped green beans with a little water and bacon grease. Cook over low heat about 1 hour. Cook broccoli and cauliflower until tender. Pour off liquid. Melt cheese and pour over broccoli and cauliflower.

Serve with a good mixed salad.

Red-Eye Gravy

Fry one slice of sugar-cured ham. Remove ham. If there are not at least 2 tablespoons of drippings, add some butter. Add a cup of strong coffee, salt and pepper to taste. Delicious with ham and eggs, toast or biscuits.

(from my mother, Mrs. Eva Slaughter)

Brother Schaap's Favorite Rutabagas

    1 or 2 rutabagas, peeled and cut up

    3 tablespoons sugar

    ½ teaspoon salt

    1 stick of butter or margarine

Cover the rutabagas with water and bring to a boil. Lower temperature to simmer. Add sugar, salt, and butter. Cook until very tender, about 1½ hours. Boil the liquid down until almost gone. Serve.

I like to cook the rutabagas the day before for more flavor.

Southern Fried Corn

    6 large cobs of corn

    3/4 cup water

    ½ stick margarine or butter

    1 teaspoon salt

    1 tablespoon sugar

    Pepper to taste

Remove the corn from the cob. Scrape the milk off the cob and put in skillet. Add water and margarine or butter. Boil. Simmer 5 to 10 minutes on low heat. Add salt, sugar, and pepper.

Sweet Potato Casserole

    3 cups cooked sweet potatoes, mashed*

    1 cup sugar

    1 stick margarine

    2 eggs, beaten

    1 teaspoon vanilla

    1/3 cup milk

Mix all ingredients. Put into lightly greased baking dish, 9x13 inches.

Topping:

    1 cup brown sugar

    ½ cup flour

    1/3 cup margarine, melted

    1 cup pecans, chopped

Mix together the topping ingredients and crumble over potato mixture. Bake at 350° for 25 minutes.

I bake about 5 medium potatoes until tender. I also use more than one cup of chopped pecans.

Hamburger Stew

1 pound ground chuck
1 small package mixed vegetables
4 cups water
1 can stewed tomatoes
Salt and pepper to taste
Rice, cooked

Brown hamburger (add minced onion if desired). Add water, tomatoes, salt, and pepper. Simmer about 30 minutes. Serve in bowls over cooked rice. Serves 4 generously.

14

Southern Grace
Is Being a Woman of Schedule

*B*everly Hyles has always been a scheduled lady. I believe that schedule is one of the primary ways to live one's life according to proper priorities. My father has been quoted as saying, "Unless you have a set time to do the big things, you will spend your life doing little things." Mom has had a way of balancing and achieving excellence in every area of her life. She especially achieved excellence in the area of being a wife, a mother, and a homemaker.

The following are some ways that my mother organized a scheduled life.

1. Beverly Hyles has gotten up early and at the same time each day. Any woman who is struggling with discipline in the art of homemaking must learn to set and to obey an alarm clock. There is no way around following this basic habit of good character. By the time I arose each morning (and I was not generally a late sleeper), my mother had already prepared a good breakfast. Breakfast was generally served at the same time each morning.

On Scheduling Your Time…

❧

We are all equal in the amount of time we have.

❧

If you never have time for you, you will become resentful.

— Beverly Hyles

2. Beverly Hyles has a habit of going to bed at the same time each evening. Growing up in the home of Beverly Hyles, I noticed that she began to get ready for bed at the same time each evening. She also allowed for some scheduled decompressing time for things such as reading and light snacking before she went to bed. My mother usually got about eight hours of sleep a night, an amount of sleep which most women require. Good health is achieved in part by scheduled rest because the body adjusts to consistent patterns of sleep.

3. Beverly Hyles has established regularly scheduled eating times. Mom's mealtimes and even snack times were scheduled. I recall my mother's taking an afternoon coffee break at approximately the same time daily.

My father arrived home from work each day at 5:00 p.m., like clockwork. He too was a very scheduled person. I recall dinner always being on the table at exactly the same time my dad arrived home. Our family would sit around the table and eat a hearty meal, while chatting about the day's events.

Much has been said recently about the importance of families eating together around the table. This is a practice that has become almost obsolete. Yet this was a practice that was scheduled consistently into our family life, especially when my three siblings and I were children.

My mom has said in her own words, "Make much of a mealtime. Make them on time and make them happy times. Plan meals to your husband's schedule."

4. Beverly Hyles was scheduled in her time with God. Her regular time of Bible reading and prayer was in the morning between breakfast and her grooming time.

5. Beverly Hyles was disciplined in her grooming routines. Mom was always ready early in the day. I don't remember her ever staying in her robe all day or even part of the day. Mom's hair, makeup, and clothing were always neatly ordered at the beginning of the day. Her practice was to get herself ready directly after breakfast and her Bible time. Mom's habits were so consistent that they were easily detectable by her children.

6. Beverly Hyles was disciplined in her weekly schedule. Monday was Mom's housecleaning day. She rarely missed a week of

On Determining Your Priorities...

Give quality time to things that are important!

❧

First, God

❧

Second, husband

❧

Third, children

❧

Fourth, yourself

❧

Fifth, home

❧

Sixth, service outside the home

– Beverly Hyles

thoroughly cleaning the house. For the first 25 years of my own marriage, I cleaned my house thoroughly every Monday. Why? Because that was how my mother did it! In my counseling, I find so many women who struggle with home organization, and the simple concept of scheduling a weekly chore seems foreign to them. Yet because of my mother's example, I found it easy not only to schedule a weekly time for chores, but also to schedule them similarly to the way my mother did. For example, some ladies grocery shop once or twice a month. Some ladies grocery shop when they get around to it. I have always grocery shopped once a week on the same day each week because that is how my mother did it.

7. **Beverly Hyles has been scheduled in her time for others.** Friday was Mom's time to go soul winning and visiting in the nursing homes. Mom was a Sunday school teacher for nearly 40 years, and in spite of a busy schedule, my mother rarely ever missed a church service or a church choir practice.

8. **Beverly Hyles adhered to a simple schedule.** Mom never scheduled herself so fully that it caused any one part of her schedule to suffer. My mother kept her schedule so that she could achieve excellence in every scheduled area. She never overloaded her schedule. Mom even scheduled times of decompression, fun and relaxation, so that her busy schedule never left her feeling frazzled for her family. She rewarded herself for tasks accomplished by planning something to look forward to after small domestic goals had been reached.

9. **Beverly Hyles planned her schedule around her husband and children.** Most of Mom's work was done while

we were not home, making her life appear not only excellent, but also effortless. Mom was very good about controlling things such as counseling, socializing, and the telephone. These things were kept to a minimum when her husband and children were home. My mother has said that she did not feel guilty cancelling things to be with her family.

Mom was known by her friends and fellow workers as being one who left meetings early because she had to be home when her children arrived home from school. She kept faithful to this practice even when I as the youngest child was the only one left at home. All the way into my high school and college years, I could count on my mother's being home when I got home from school.

I have taught college-age young ladies for 24 years. I have known many sweet Christian girls who seem unable to excel in their college years. These ladies want to do right and succeed. They may love God more than other girls who seem to prosper in their academics. But no one taught these girls how to organize their time.

I also work with the wives of married college men. These wives frequently ask advice about how to organize their homes and their time. They are looking for some easy and unique answer. The answers to an organized home and life are neither easy or unique. If a young lady would follow the simple principles listed in this chapter, she could effectively acquire an organized home and life as much as anyone else can. Yet these simple principles are foreign to many. They have not been taught these principles, nor have they seen them by example in their own mother's life.

I am thankful for a mother who not only taught me how to organize my time, but also made me an important part of her schedule and priority list. I am thankful for a mother who was always there when I got home from school and who provided mealtimes that were happy times.

I am thankful for a mother who lived a simply scheduled life according to proper priorities.

On Scheduling…

As much as possible, get up and go to bed
at the same time every day.

Eat at regular times and have good eating habits.

Establish your grooming routines.

Schedule prayer and Bible reading times.

Read a portion of a book and the newspaper daily.

Take a 10 to 15 minute walk daily, if only around your yard.

— Beverly Hyles

15

Southern Grace
Is a Celebration!

*S*outhern Grace is a celebration—a traditional celebration! I could not write about either one of my parents without including their love for holidays.

Christmas started with our quad-level house being decorated like a fairy land. As a child, I loved to go from room to room and stare at the many Christmas decorations my mother had accumulated through the years. Mom decorated to the maximum. Had she been heavily involved in a career, I doubt she would have had time to make Christmas as unforgettable as she did. Christmas would have been a rush and a hassle, and our memories would be hit or miss. As it is, some of my favorite memories from childhood are those of the holidays. I don't know if it is because the events were so grand, or if it was because they were so traditional and predictable that they are forever etched in my brain!

On Christmas Eve, Dad would read the Christmas story in Luke 2, we would pray, and then my parents, my three siblings, and I would open several gifts one person at a time, savoring every moment of the holiday and stretching it out as far as we could. Mom always had some kind of delicious buffet, which included Christmas cookies that my sisters and I would bake with her. (If you knew how messy I was, you would be amazed I was even allowed in the kitchen.)

All of the wrapped presents opened on Christmas Eve were from Mom and Dad. And they were beautifully wrapped, I might add! When we went to bed on Christmas Eve, Mom and Dad would begin to fill the stockings hung on the fireplace and to place unwrapped presents under the tree. Those presents were from Santa Claus. I hesitate to mention Santa Claus in this book because many people hate the tradition of Santa. My father, however, loved the fable of Santa Claus. Dad was closer to God than most anyone I knew, and so I will allow him this "vice." Dad died at 74. On one of his last Christmases, he bought my mother Santa Claus dishes, Santa Claus glasses, Santa Claus mugs, Santa Claus placemats, Santa Claus lampshades and Santa Claus chair covers…and well, you get the picture. Dad was a kid at heart. My father loved Santa Claus, and my mother followed my father.

Some of my favorite memories with my sister Linda are of our taking turns going to the bathroom on Christmas Eve. We shared a bedroom for awhile that was at the end of a long hallway on the upstairs floor. The bathroom, however, was at the top of the stairs and had a clear view of the living room and the Christmas tree. "I just went to the bathroom; now it's your turn," I would tell my sister, and she would make her way to the top of the stair to see what "Santa Claus" had brought us. Most of our lives we were well aware that Mom and Dad were the real Santa Claus and Mrs. Santa, and oh, what a wonderful pair they were!

Christmas morning began with a huge Southern breakfast which consisted of items such as scrambled eggs with cheese, creamed gravy with biscuits, Canadian bacon, and redeye gravy. My mother prepared a hot breakfast every morning with more than one food item, but Christmas morning was extra special! Mom excelled as a cook, and her breakfasts were one of her specialties. I especially loved her red-eye gravy served over ham, Canadian bacon, or toast.

After breakfast my siblings and I were allowed to view our gifts from "Santa Claus." We took our time viewing our gifts once more. Then Mom went back to work preparing Christmas dinner. What a glorious dinner we had!

New Year's Day had various traditions, but we could always count on another glorious dinner from Mom. Thanksgiving dinner was just as glorious, with all of the traditional trimmings. The Easter bunny always came at Easter, leaving us many candy eggs to be hunted and placed in our Easter baskets.

And then there were our birthdays! I don't recall ever having a birthday as a child without having a party, usually with several friends coming to our house. The games were traditional, such as "pin the tail on the donkey" and "drop the clothespins in the bottle." Dad was always there to "ham" it up during the games, and a homemade birthday cake as well as other snacks graced the dining room table. Home movies were taken, which I enjoyed viewing later in life. No matter how old I became, I don't remember ever feeling forgotten on my birthday.

So why include a chapter about Christmas and birthdays in a book called *Southern Grace*? What does this have to do with who my mother is? It has everything to do with who my mother is. Had my Mom been disinterested or selfish in her role as wife and mother, or had she been heavily involved in a career, many of these events would never have taken place as they did. Many traditions would have fallen by the wayside, and some would never have become traditions at all. Most of my favorite childhood memories—the memories that remind me who I am— would not have happened.

Of course, it wasn't until I was an adult with children of my own that I realized how much work the holidays had been for my mom. Christmas was a day off for my father, a time to play for the children, and a season of much added work for my mother. What goes around comes around, and I am now the one who does most of the holiday work around my house. But I do it gladly. I do it gladly because I had a wonderful example of how to teach a family to love life. I had a wonderful example of how to make life a celebration—a traditional celebration!

Southern Grace:
A Biographical Sketch

Beverly Hyles, 1989

16

Southern Grace
Is Being a Fundamental Lady

"*Who can find a virtuous woman? for her price is far above rubies.*" (Proverbs 31:10)

Beverly Joyce Slaughter was born on an appropriate day for such a feminine lady—Valentine's Day, February 14, 1929. Beverly was born in the Florence Nightingale Hospital of Dallas, Texas. She was born to parents who were already in their thirties: Clarence Mallory (C.M.) and Eva Slaughter. She had an older brother whom they called Buddy. He was five years old at the time of his sister's birth.

Beverly was born to a family that was already comfortably well-to-do. Her father owned a feed store, and the family lived in a comfortable home in a middle-class neighborhood.

Though Beverly's father did not go to church, her mother took Beverly to the East Grand Baptist Church, a large Southern Baptist church, and enrolled her in Sunday school when she was just three weeks old.

Beverly lived a very stable life. She moved at the age of three to Harlandale Street in Dallas. Beverly lived in this home until she married. Her parents lived there until they were old and unable to care for themselves.

Clarence Mallory Slaughter was an affectionate father, though he refused to attend church very often with his family. He had been sprinkled as a Methodist, and he claimed that was good enough for him. Eva Slaughter was a rather quiet and not openly affectionate woman, but she showed her concern for her family in the way she cared for them. She was an excellent housekeeper and cook. She sewed dresses for her daughter all the years Beverly lived at home. Many of Beverly's dresses were made out of old feed sacks, but they were lovely. Beverly hardly ever owned a store-bought dress.

Shortly after the family moved to Harlandale, Beverly, whom her family affectionately called "Sis," fell and split her knee to the bone. She was laid up so long that she had to learn to walk again after her leg healed. Beverly's mom moved her bed beside a window so she could look out and see what was happening outside. Eva Slaughter created some wonderful memories for her daughter by the way she cared for her at this time.

The fact that her mother was an excellent hostess added to Beverly's happiness as a child. Many of her father's relatives would gather at her house for holidays. Eva Slaughter set a good example of both accepting and spoiling her husband's family. Clarence's brother Eric was a fat, jolly bachelor who often came to visit and whom Beverly loved dearly.

Another of Clarence's brothers, Jim, and his wife Gertie were dear to Beverly. She loved to spend time in their beautiful home. Uncle Jim was a Cadillac dealer, but he was also active in the First Methodist Church, a fairly good church at that time.

Occasionally, Beverly would visit her mother's parents. Eva's mother was a heavyset woman with many health problems, and for that reason, Beverly did not get to see her often. Eva's father was a very fun-loving man, and Beverly enjoyed very much her occasional visits with him.

When the Slaughter family moved to Harlandale Street, they transferred their membership to the Hillcrest Baptist Church. Again, let me mention that theirs was a stable life. Hillcrest Baptist Church was the only church Beverly attended from this time until she married. This church was where Beverly would meet her future husband.

Beverly loved her guitar-playing, football-playing older brother, Buddy. At the age of nine, Beverly's brother walked the aisle for salvation. Beverly followed him. One of the workers at the altar filled out a slip saying that Beverly was saved, but no one actually went over the plan of salvation with her. Though she was baptized with her brother that same evening, Beverly had not been truly saved.

A week later Beverly sat in the bathtub preparing to go to a picture show. Suddenly, she was convicted that it was a sin to go to the movies. She promised God then and there she would not attend the movie. She also realized for the first time that she was a sinner, and she asked Jesus to save her there in the bathtub. That same summer Beverly went forward during Vacation Bible School and surrendered to full-time Christian service.

The teachers had been telling missionary stories each day

during Bible school, and my mom dedicated her life to become a missionary to Africa. She did not realize it, but her future husband would do the same thing during his young life. Though the paths of their future would take them in a much different direction, there is no doubt in my mind that God was already preparing them for something special.

After her salvation, Beverly's life began to agree with Jack's in one way, though there were few similarities. She also began to build her life around the church. Beverly never missed a Sunday, and she became a champion at memorizing the Bible, first in the city of Dallas and then at the Texas state capital.

Beverly often walked to church alone on Sunday evenings and Wednesday evenings because her mother stayed home with her father. She was taught to tithe on her income. Her mother always gave her an offering to take to church.

As just a junior girl, Beverly climbed trees, where she sat and dreamed of being a singer. (Would you believe such a fundamental lady was ever a tomboy?) Beverly became involved in a junior girls' trio and sang in church quite often. One trio member was Libby Sumrall, the pastor's daughter. Because of Beverly's friendship with Libby, she spent much time in the pastor's home. Beverly loved Pastor Sumrall and his family. She loved the pastor's wife, in particular, who was a pretty woman and a gracious hostess. She made being a pastor's wife look good to Beverly.

When Beverly was a young teenager, she and Libby Sumrall formed a trio with Marguerite Stevenson, who was used by God to encourage my dad to go forward and to surrender to preach.

Music would become the main interest which God used to keep Mom involved in the church—more involved than the rest of her family. God used the music director, Mr. Browning, in her life at this time also.

Beverly was greatly influenced by her teachers at Hillcrest Baptist Church. She remembers in particular Mrs. Littlepage, Mrs. Rusek, and Mrs. Howard. Mrs. Howard was the mother of one of my dad's close friends, Leroy Howard.

Not only did Beverly enjoy church, but she also enjoyed school. She attributes her first grade teacher, Mrs. Goldsmith, as being the one who got her off to a good start in school. Mrs. Goldsmith was an old maid schoolteacher who made school exciting. Beverly became and stayed a straight "A" student. My mom went to the same junior high school as did my father. Though they were there at different times, they had many of the same teachers.

Beverly continued to like and enjoy school, but her enthusiasm waned a little bit as she found a new interest—boys. She grew to her full height in junior high. At the age of 13, she was almost 5' 8", and she was very interested in boys. She was already beautiful, and she would often walk by the house of a boy named Jack Hyles. She did not realize that he was noticing her. He often thought to himself how lovely she was. He wished that she were older and that he were taller.

Again, my mother's childhood was very different from my father's. It was almost as stable as his was unstable; but like my father, my mom did not fit in well at school. Most of her friends were from her church.

Mom attended a different high school from Dad. Dad went to Adamson High School, and Mom attended Sunset High School. What stands out in her mind about high school days is the fact that she had two teachers who pointed out her special abilities in both music and art. Mom chose to pursue music over art, and I believe that God was in that choice. Though my mom has become a wonderful artist in the last few decades, it is her music that has spiritually blessed the hearts of her husband's congregations. My mother's lovely and compassionate singing voice was a most fitting, yet useful, decoration on the foundation of my father's ministry. I cannot imagine the fundamental lady, my mother, without her beautiful voice.

Not only does Mom have a beautiful voice, but she also has a dedicated voice. To use her voice for the Lord is a decision she made in high school. She came to that decision the hard way. During high school, Beverly sang in both the church and school choirs, and she often sang at assemblies and at the teen canteen. On one particular occasion, she was chosen to represent Sunset High School at an all-city program at the teen canteen. A dance was to follow the program; and though Beverly planned to leave before the dance, she knew that she had no business being there. Beverly got up to sing and could not remember her words. She went behind a curtain where others encouraged her to go out and try again. She tried again and forgot her words a second time. She tried a third time and forgot the words again. Finally, she sang another more familiar song. The audience was laughing, and among those laughing was a young man named Jack Hyles. The following Sunday, an embarrassed and more humble

Beverly went forward at the Hillcrest Baptist Church. She then promised God that she would give her voice to sing for Him. She would not use her talent for the world.

In high school Beverly went steady with a football star named Charlie Dickerson. Charlie was a member of the Church of Christ. He was not really a bad boy, but he was not a good boy either. He claimed to be saved, but he would not attend the Baptist church with Beverly.

One evening Beverly attended the Church of Christ with Charlie and his mother. She felt very uncomfortable and knew that she did not agree with what was being taught. She also realized something else—Charlie Dickerson was not saved. With that realization, she began to feel convicted about ending their steady relationship. Ending that relationship opened the door to my mother's dating Jack Hyles.

What has stood out about my mother's early life as I have studied for this chapter is the following:

1. *She had a life which led her to Fundamentalism.* Not only was her life a stable one, but it was a life built around the church. It was a life filled with the fiery preaching of her second pastor at Hillcrest, Pastor Sisemore. It was a life where my mother began an early commitment to Christ and to doing right.

2. *She had a life which led her to femininity.* My mother has always been to me exactly what a lady should be. As I have learned about her early life, I have discovered the reason for her femininity. I believe the reason for my mother's femininity can be described in two words: role models.

The first role model I will mention was her pastor's wife, Mrs. Sumrall. She was the gracious and pretty hostess who made being a pastor's wife look good.

Secondly, let me mention the church organist, who was a very faithful young lady named Luella. She was only five or six years older than my mother. My mother admired her as a beautiful young woman who was obviously committed to the Lord.

Thirdly, let me mention the church secretary, who often wrote notes to my mother. One note said something like this: *"I think God is going to use you someday."*

Last of all, but not least, was my maternal grandmother, Eva Slaughter. She was a quiet and a private woman; therefore, she was not easy to get to know. However, she was an old- fashioned homemaker, and she very effectively passed on this trait to her only daughter. Eva Slaughter was committed to caring for her family.

Eva taught her little "Sis" to be faithful to church. She not only taught her to attend church, but she sent an offering with her each week. One of my father's earliest memories of their marriage is of Mom making him give their last twenty dollars to the Lord because they had not yet tithed. It was Eva Slaughter who taught my mother to give.

Mamaw Slaughter, as I called her, taught my mother to love the Bible. Mamaw usually read through the Bible more than once a year. After Mamaw's death, we found in her Bible a record of the many times she had read through the Bible.

Mamaw taught my mother how to be a submissive help meet to her husband. Though Mamaw read the Bible through at least once each year, she never read the Bible when her unsaved husband was home. Though she was faithful to attend church each Sunday morning, she was not privileged to become involved in the other services and activities of the church. She stayed at home with her husband. She did not preach the Christian life to her husband; she lived it before him by serving him and his family, and eventually her husband became a Christian.

My mother has always been dedicated to doing what God wanted her to do. She has been fundamentally dedicated to His will for her life and her talents.

Mom has always been most fundamentally a lady. She is as fundamentally feminine as my father was masculine. She is the gracious hostess, as was her pastor's wife, Mrs. Sumrall. She is the beautiful and consecrated musician, as was Luella. She has been the encouraging note writer, as was the church secretary. She has been the spiritual help meet, as was her own mother. What she did best was to stand in the background and allow my father to make his own spiritual decisions. Her Christian life has been a quiet, yet consistent one. As her mother before her, she did not try to lead her husband spiritually.

I am thankful for my mother's role models and for what they have helped her to become. Beverly Joyce Slaughter Hyles has become a wonderful role model to thousands of women, and she is mine.

Cindy Schaap and Beverly Hyles
2008

Conclusion

$\mathcal{A}$s a pastor's wife, far too frequently women come to my office to share with me the past hurts of their childhood. Some subjects are not too serious, yet are nevertheless hurtful. Statements are made such as:

- "My mother was rarely home."
- "My mother never taught me to keep house."
- "My mother kept a messy house, and I never had an example in this area."
- "My mother never kept a schedule."
- "My mother stayed in bed a lot."
- "We never ate dinner together as a family."
- "We never celebrated birthdays or holidays."

Others are very serious:

- "My mother never told me she loved me."
- "My mother didn't want me."
- "My mother left me, my dad, and my siblings."
- "My mother is unsaved."
- "My mother tried to abort me."

- "My mother abused me."
- "My mother brought boyfriends into the home."
- "My mother was sexually promiscuous."

Rarely a week goes by, if not a day, when I do not think to myself, "I never had to think about these problems as a child, much less deal with them. Thank You, Lord, for my mother."

And then I often ask myself, "Does my mother know how blessed I feel that she is my mother?"

This book has been an attempt, not only to tell you what a great mother I had and to set her forth as an example but also to express my gratitude for what I have not suffered in my life…because of my mother.

This book is a chance to say "thank you," not only to my mom, but also to my God Who spared me so much tragedy…because of the heritage He has given me.

Psalm 16:6, *"The lines are fallen unto me in pleasant places; yea, I have a goodly heritage."*

Psalm 61:5, *"…thou hast given me the heritage of those that fear thy name."*

James 1:17, *"Every good gift and every perfect gift is from above, and cometh down from the Father of lights, with whom is no variableness, neither shadow of turning."*

Proverbs 31:28, *"Her children arise up, and call her blessed…."*

———

And Mom and I would add together:

Ephesians 3:21, *"Unto him* [God] *be glory in the church by Christ Jesus throughout all ages, world without end. Amen."*

Appendix

*A*s a conclusion to this book, I would like to list some of my mother's accomplishments in the area of writing, preparing messages for ladies, and recording music.

At this writing, Beverly Hyles has written four books and one booklet:

I Feel Precious to God
Life, As Viewed From the Goldfish Bowl
Marred Vessels in the Potter's Hands
Woman, the Assembler
You Are Somebody

A pictorial flipbook with the quotations of both my parents has been produced entitled *A Voice: The Quotations of Dr. Jack Hyles ~ A Vessel: The Quotations of Beverly Hyles.*

Through the years, 29 messages by my mother have been recorded and produced by Christian Womanhood:

"Are You Sitting at Home While Your Husband Is at Work?" (Resenting Your Husband's Church Work)

"At Home Where You Belong"

"Bringing Order to Your Topsy-Turvy World"

"Celebrate You"

"Depression and the Christian Woman"

"Furnace of Affliction"

"Gaining Victory Over Depression"

"God's Old-Fashioned Strange Ways"

"Help With Weight Control"

"Home Is a Person"

"How to Avoid Burnout"

"I Am a Miracle! You Are a Miracle!"

"Is It Stormy? Look for a Rainbow!"

"Ladies Who Have Helped Me Be a Pastor's Wife"

"Learning to Love Yourself"

"Life's Inescapables"

"Making Your Husband Feel Like a King"

"Please Don't Have a Nervous Breakdown"

"Satan's Carousel—Help for Discouragement"

"Stop Being Mad at Yourself"

"Ten P's for a Happy Marriage"

"The Abundant Life"

"Twenty Ways to Stay on Top"

"What Is Your Heart Posture?"

"What to Do When You Are at Your Wit's End"

"You're Simply Marvelous!"

"You Are Somebody"

"Your Choice: Purity or Death"

My mother has made seven vocal music recordings. The first two recordings were long-play records:

"Jesus Is the Sweetest Name I Know"

"Sunrise…Sunset" (duets with Ed Wolber)

Christian Womanhood asked Mom to make a vocal music cassette in 1988. She would make four more in the next five years. Those titles are:

"Some of My Favorites—Old and New"

"The Sun Will Shine Again"

"Seasons of Life~Ecclesiastes 3:1-8"

"Rejoice!" (Songs of Christ and Christmas)

"From Our Homes to Yours" (duets with Ed Wolber)

Mom chose 24 of my dad's and her favorite songs from the five vocal music cassettes, and Christian Womanhood produced a double CD of these songs entitled "Some of Our Favorites!"

Most of these materials are still available from Christian Womanhood, 8400 Burr Street, Crown Point, Indiana 46307.